ALCHEMIZING EXPLOITATION

Alchemizing Exploitation

SARAH LAUREN

TABLE OF CONTENTS

~ 1 ~

THE FACTS

The Department of Defense reports 4.5 million people worldwide are victims of forced sexual exploitation. 1 in 6 endangered runaways in the U.S. is likely to become a sex trafficking victim. The U.S. Department of State estimates that approximately 17,500 foreign nationals are trafficked into the United States annually. Reports made to the U.S. National Human Trafficking Hotline in 2021 found 16,544 victims of human trafficking in the United States. Of these known cases, employers trafficked 43%, family members trafficked 26%, and intimate partners trafficked 22%[1]. On top of those staggering numbers and statistics, sex trafficking is under-reported, making it difficult to know the actual number of victims.

In 2023, the movie "The Sound of Freedom" was released to the public. In the credits, they left the audience with this thought:

"Human trafficking is a 150 billion dollar a year business. The United States is one of the top destinations for human trafficking and is among the largest consumers of child sex. There are more humans trapped in slavery today than at any other time in history – including when slavery was legal. Millions of these slaves are children."

I am beyond grateful to those who fight against this travesty to rescue the enslaved worldwide. As a survivor, I seek to answer certain questions about this issue that others might not. What if someone who was enslaved wasn't kidnapped or detained but coerced into selling sex? How can we empower the sexually exploited to walk out after they have the freedom to walk out? How do we help them realize they can live free? Once freedom is achieved, how do we help each other heal from what happened?

I wrote this story to bring awareness to those enduring sexual exploitation in our culture. People of different backgrounds have experienced sexual exploitation without realizing what was happening, and it's not like the movies. A 19-year-old girl in Iowa, trying to make sense of the broken pieces of her life after trusting the wrong guy. A girl who doesn't talk to family or friends she grew up with because of debilitating shame. One who allowed the allure of something new, different, or hopeful, to interfere with their safety. Maybe someone else allowed uncomfortable situations to please a boyfriend. Others made a bad judgment call.

Imagine, someone promised you your heart's desire, and you don't know that there's a price. A big price. You don't know it will permanently alter the course of your life. Having your body commodified is excruciating for the soul. Teenagers running away from home are among the most vulnerable. Kids growing up in the foster care system are another high-risk category. Worldwide,women and children suffer from trauma that stems from sexual exploitation. It has permeated modern society and spread like wildfire right under our feet. When a person in captivity who has been sex trafficked does break free, the trauma often affects their lives forever. Millions around the globe have been affected and are desperately searching for wholeness. I believe this wholeness is attainable. The more we, the trafficked, share the truth about the reality of what is happening and how it has affected our lives, the more people are empowered to rise above the shame they feel. If one person affected by this cancer gets the slightest glimmer of hope from my story, I've succeeded.

It's terrifying to think of how insidious this modern-day slavery has become. Violating young men, women, and children in a way they don't understand goes on to present the extreme challenge of understanding what happened to them and how to recover. Stepping out of fear is vital to our individual and collective well-being. I hope anyone trapped in fear will experience liberation.

Personally, I grew up fearing knowledge. There wasn't any discussion or acknowledgment of sex in my house. It was embarrassing to even *think* of my anatomy. Lack of education about the topic was a contributing factor to the situation I was in as a teenager. Many people have had similar experiences. I've had to overcome a lot of fear-based thinking to share this story. I feared speaking up and potentially creating a controversy by discussing something most people see as extremely taboo. In my experience, overcoming fear gives birth to miracles. Storytelling has been used to illuminate places of darkness for thousands of years. Amidst challenges over the last few years, authentic voices are rising to the surface, encouraging all of us. I've healed enough to know it's okay to show the world the depths of my soul. Everyone should be able to do so. Depth is not something to fear. It's something to be celebrated. As I embrace my depths, I find my voice and offer my story to those who need it. This message is for them. Maybe, it's for you.

Millions of men, women, and children across the globe are being sexually exploited. Right now. Many of them don't know what's happening or how to stop it. Some have escaped but have forgotten who they are. Sex trafficking is a tremendous problem, but there is a way to stop it. Every survivor who makes it out can heal. This happens when we remember who we are and where we belong. I hope to help other survivors remember. This is how we rescue each other. We have to remind one another of our vast resources and share that knowledge. This movement will continue to affect transformation in our culture as we awaken to the truths of our shared reality. When Jesus healed the sick man by the pool, he told him to pick up his mat and walk. It's the same with every person trapped in industries that exploit them. We can all pick up our mats and walk. So much in life reminds us of who we are and where we belong. Thoughtful words, kind gestures, beautiful music, ancient texts, and mindful practices all echo the same truth.

Nobody can take away peace from someone who knows who they are. No matter how long we have forgotten or how far we have gone, it's time to remember. This book explores the ways I remembered and reclaimed my true self. I hope it's helpful to anyone just behind me on their journey, looking for a way out. The more I connect with others who've had similar experiences, the lighter I feel. We help each other. The community unfolding out of sharing, understanding, and healing has created a safe place.

Through connection with each other and truth, we can collectively wake up to the truth that we are not for sale. I believe people who have lived through the most horrific nightmares have the deepest propensity for joy. As a community of survivors, we are alchemizing the collective through our stories of healing. Thanks to everyone who has embraced this path with me. Oxford defines the word transmute as "completely transforming, especially into something different and better."

I'm looking forward to transmuting more dark places in our society with our growing community of survivors.

~ 2 ~

THE DARK DAYS

MY STORY

At 18, I reconnected with my biological mother. Before I became legally recognized as an adult, I took it upon myself to find out the truth about what happened to her. Wondering why she wasn't in my life haunted me from the time she left when I was 5 years old. For a couple of years after my adoption, we exchanged letters. She would send birthday and Christmas cards with different addresses and sometimes different last names. In my search, I found a few of her marriage certificates. She was married 6 times. I sent letters to all her addresses with my contact number. When I got the call from her responding to my last letter, it surprised me to learn she was only a 30-minute drive away. I still remember shaking with excitement when I heard her voice on the other end of my silver flip phone. The moment she spoke, I knew it was her. She invited me to come over the very next morning.

The familiar buzz of a city apartment building gate unlatching rang in my ears as I walked up the narrow stairwell to the second floor. It smelled like cigarette smoke and stale liquor.

Just as I reached the corner apartment, the door opened before I could knock. Joyce appeared and greeted me. She was grinning from ear to ear as she hugged and kissed me. Her baggy dress reached the floor, covered at the top with a red lace cardigan. Three long necklaces were bunched together around her chest. The beads dug into me somewhat painfully as we embraced. I smiled back and said, 'Hi, Joyce'. I didn't know what to call her, but felt like I'd always known her. Her green eyes sparkled over her freckled face. She took me by the hand and led me into her smoky living room, where her most recent husband greeted me. He was a tall Jordanian man, and his glasses rested on his nose. He expressed his gratitude for the reconnection.

We talked for hours about the last thirteen years. Joyce had tried to call me when we moved away after the adoption, she said. She explained it was an open adoption, and my family wasn't supposed to stop her from talking to me. She seemed very hurt, like they had tricked her and kidnapped me. Her face was shaking with emotion as she recalled the events. I felt sorry for her. Her red lipstick stressed the wrinkles around her mouth. A thick scrunchie held her thinning hair in a high ponytail. Joyce remarked on how beautiful I was several times, followed by a description of herself at my age. She mentioned she was a size 5, and men frequently followed her around the block. I laughed. She seemed down to earth and not afraid to speak her mind—a stark contrast to the calm and collected family that nurtured me from birth.

Joyce and I spent time together at her apartment over the next few months. It felt good to bond with the mother I'd lost. She told me all about her life. She described her childhood experiences while growing up in the foster care system. Telling me stories of being thrown out of a second-story window, stories about running away from evil foster homes and working on the streets of New York. Joyce told me about her hard life and what she did to survive growing up. It was no big deal selling sex for money, she said. She had to. It didn't last long. This nonchalant attitude towards selling herself made the whole concept of prostitution seem normal. Today, I recognize this as grooming.

By 19 years old, my mother had trafficked me into the sex industry. I can't remember who, how, or when it happened. That memory is still inaccessible to me, no matter how hard I try to come up with it. To say that I was naive would be an understatement. Religious beliefs that my family had raised me with excused me from health class in high school. Lacking a working knowledge of sex, drugs, or alcohol, I didn't know how they affected my body. I didn't know what methamphetamines were when I took a hit. All I knew was what Joyce told me when she handed me a pipe and lighter after demonstrating.

"It will make you feel good, baby."

The blackouts started immediately, as days turned into weeks and weeks turned into months. Joyce called her city apartment "the candy store," where I could find many exotic substances to assist in limitless adventures. She reminded me often that the world was my oyster, and I could do whatever I wanted whenever I liked. The picture of freedom she painted was exhilarating, as were her offerings. MDMA, angel dust, morphine, cocaine, methamphetamines, and ecstasy pills.

I can vividly recall one instance in which my head was clearing from whatever concoction of drugs someone had served me maybe a week prior. The lack of any ability to recall anything for days tells me the key ingredient was probably GHB. I was in a studio apartment in the avenues of San Francisco. From the inside, I didn't know where I was. There was a king-sized bed, a small bathroom, and a kitchenette. The dirty, cluttered space was littered with discarded food, empty bottles, and piles of clothes. I passed a man and a woman, both asleep on the bed. I couldn't find a door to leave. Turning on the bathroom light, I tried not to disturb the strangers. They hadn't moved. When I saw the door, I noticed with horror it was boarded and nailed shut. I don't remember how I got from inside that studio into the glaring daylight of the morning. Somehow, I did. With my purse and phone in hand, I walked down the avenue toward Golden Gate Park and called my sister. My family didn't know what happened. I didn't either. Somehow, I'd caught a ride straight to hell. I needed help, or I was going to die. Within weeks, a safe house for women escaping their traffickers accepted me into their program. I will always be thankful for those six months.

The safe house provided me with a life-saving introduction to recovery. However, I viewed it as temporary, not a lifelong commitment. I didn't understand the long-term consequences of what I'd just lived. I wasn't slowing down enough to feel that yet. Despite loving care and support from the beautiful women who ran that home, I didn't last. My first bout of rage completely blindsided me. I was simply walking down the street on a sunny day when my body started burning. Without thinking, I picked up an empty garbage can from the curb and threw it into the middle of the street. Shaking in anger, I stood staring in shock as hot tears rolled down my cheeks. Three days later, I was on an airplane to Boston. I left the full scholarship to a music school the safe house had granted me behind. This was the second of many life-changing opportunities I ran away from.

TRAUMA

It turns out that outrage is a natural but extreme response to infringing boundaries. In a 2022 interview with Tim Ferriss, Dr. Gabor Maté, an expert in trauma, explains, "If your boundaries were infringed upon as a child, but you could not express it, it didn't disappear. It gets suppressed. It becomes like a volcano gurgling and bubbling inside you, but has no expression."[2] My boundaries had certainly been infringed upon. I didn't understand it then, but now I can see why I was prone to explosions of rage. Throughout the course of my life, minor events triggered this rage. Now, when it happens, I can recognize it as a response to the past. By fully allowing myself to experience the biological process of rage, I can nurture myself into a calm state.

The trauma of having my body exploited for sex played out in my life for years. For a decade, I cycled through patterns of anger, avoidance, and isolation. I was ashamed, identifying my experiences with who I was. When I felt a burst of rage coming, it was easy enough for me to jump on an airplane and leave whatever area of the country I was living in. I only knew how to escape. Though I had gotten out of that situation with Joyce, I was far from healed.

At 20 years old, my rage controlled me. I self-medicated daily with alcohol and drugs. Having already been exposed to the adult entertainment industry, I found it to be my best option for easy money. It was easy to work and travel. I was addicted to the process. There were periods of time I spent every week in a different city. Sometimes, I left the country for months at a time, telling no one who I was with or where I was going. If I kept moving, maybe the rage wouldn't overtake me, and I could stay in the shadows. I moved through life this way for a long time, staying hidden.

Trauma is a funny thing. A prevalent curse in our modern society that we are only now facing with real wisdom. Experiencing sexual abuse at a young age without the coherence of mind to run or fight caused my brain to dissociate. This is a natural response to preserve your life. I learned to split off from my consciousness, so neural pathways in my brain were severed. It was the only way I could distance myself from the moment. Zone out. Dissociation was a coping mechanism I used for most of my life. My chameleon nature was a point of pride in my twenties. Later, I understood the pathology of such a character trait. The long-term impact of this pattern of dissociating controlled me before I began the healing process. According to psychiatrists, over the years, this manifested as PTSD and Borderline Personality Disorder.

HOW IT HAPPENS

How prevalent is the adult entertainment industry in the United States today? How about in the world? According to the French organization Fondation Scelles, there are approximately 2 million sex workers in the US alone today. Worldwide, that number jumps to 42 million, 75% of which are between the ages of 13 and 25. It's hard to imagine how common this stark reality is. The human brain fully develops at 25.

Traffickers don't always kidnap and chain people to a bed. Yes, this happens throughout the world. It's tragic to think about the women and children being used underground. It's an evil that our society at large must wake up to. However, many adult workers' exploitation started with someone they thought they could trust. That was my experience. Many women have walked a similar path.

Imagine an 18-year-old girl head over heels for a guy she wants to please. She's legally an adult, so she moves in with him, on top of the world. At first, the experience is exhilarating. Then, he pushes the limits of her boundaries, using champagne to lower her inhibitions. Life feels glamorous to her. The situation subtly changes. In a show of desperation, he tells the young girl he needs several hundred dollars for the rent. He tells her about a friend he knows who could make a thousand dollars in one brief hour. All she had to do was have fun alone time with a man. She agrees. Half-drunk, she entertains a stranger who has his way with her. As the shame washes over her in the sobering light of morning, she reaches for another drink, drowns it out, and continues down the path before her.

"Grooming" is when an adult develops a friendship with a child or vulnerable individual intending to have an illegal sexual relationship.[3] The groomer intends to manipulate the person into exploitation. The victim may not even realize they have a choice. This is how most sexual abuse begins with children and young adults. Adults acting as groomers are typically family members, caregivers, or significant others.

I believe in taking radical responsibility for my actions. This is something that comes with age, brain development, support, and maturity. A young girl immersed in an exploitative environment rarely has the wherewithal to change her circumstances or know that she needs to. An 18-year-old girl is still emotionally a child, even if they're adults in the eyes of the law in many countries. She hasn't developed the awareness to know her own power. This is especially true where trauma is present. Trauma causes brain development to stunt.

A 23-year-old survivor may only have emotionally developed to 13 years old when they were traumatized. It's important to meet sex trafficking survivors at their emotional level. Knowing how to relate to someone who looks a certain age but acts like a teenager is challenging. Others like them, who have shared experiences, help heal survivors most. Encouraging stories of hope are important both individually and collectively. Freedom and healing are possible. It's contagious. Reaching out to others trapped in their traumas has helped me make peace with the past.

SEARCHING

After exploring the world drunk, I got dizzy and stayed stationary for a while. I'd love to report that I settled down to heal. However, I wasn't ready. While I was pretending to work for an older man who traded commodities as his compliance officer, we became partners in avoidance. My "boss" and I spent our days in a sunny retirement community, visiting the pool and golf course by noon with a steady buzz from vodka cocktails. For all the fun, it was a toxic situation for both of us. He put his severe alcoholism on display for me during those months. It allowed me to look into a potential future that I didn't find very attractive.

We were in San Diego, and I remembered my mother telling me about an aunt from my father's side who lived in the area. I still wanted to know more about where I came from. My mother didn't tell me much at all about my father, so I took matters into my own hands to find him. I had the name of my aunt and knew she was an attorney. She had a unique Norwegian surname, so finding her wasn't too hard.

After a basic Google search, I found the phone number of her office and placed the call. My Aunt, Gladys, answered right away and knew exactly who I was. She was so nonchalant about talking to me like this sort of thing happened every day. We chatted for a while, and she was open to meeting, so I invited her over. Gladys, a tall blonde, came over to our condo for a visit one afternoon. She laughed at my "California family" living situation, which she immediately understood. She filled me in on the family tree and found a place for my branch. During my adoption proceedings, Gladys testified against my father (her brother), telling the court about his rage and alcoholism. They hated each other. She had considered adopting me herself, but the timing was off; she was still in law school. Gladys later told me a story about getting a guy drunk and having her friend sleep with him to get pregnant so they could have a child. This glimpse into my paternal biology didn't look promising. However, there was still a chance my father had always loved and missed me. I looked at my family tree. I had 5 siblings. Glen, my father, had been married 3 times. I was excited to learn I had a big sister, so I started there.

Mary wasn't hard to find. She worked at a doctor's office, and I called once I found the number. Mary answered the phone. Before I could tell her who I was, she asked if I was Lauren. I said yes, and she squealed with excitement, saying she had just been talking about me. Neither one of us knew exactly how she recognized my voice, but she did. I think it could be because our voices are identical. She'd just been telling a coworker about her little sister, whom she promised to find one day. When I was born, I had a different name. The morning of my adoption, I announced to my family that I would now go by the name Sarah. I was 5 years old. My family honored that and changed my name during the adoption process. I've always found that to be very gracious on their part. Mary was a few years older than me, and our brother was a couple of years older than her. They'd met me once at a supervised visit before my adoption. I only vaguely remembered it and, until this point, had thought it was a dream. Mary asked me if I remembered her promise to find me one day. I didn't, but it was a sweet moment. She was lovely, and we still keep in touch.

I planned to drive out to meet Mary in person a few weeks after we talked on the phone. She'd told me enough about our father to find him, too. He'd legally changed his name a few years back since he spent much of his early adulthood playing the con artist role. Armed with his current legal name, I looked him up on social media and sent him a friend request.

It took Roark about a week to figure out who I was and accept my request. He wrote a long post on my page about our separation and the family that was waiting for me in Louisiana. It's funny how some people don't quite grasp the lack of discretion that comes with posting on someone's public Facebook page. Regardless, I was in a state of pure ecstasy. I'd discovered my father's identity, and he wanted me! We started talking by phone, and I decided I wanted to meet him in person, too. I said goodbye to my boss and hit the road.

Meeting Mary in person was a wonderful experience. She was tall, beautiful, and sweet as can be. It turns out I was the shortest person in my newly found family. Mary towered over me with bright turquoise eyes like the Caribbean sea. It was the first time I'd ever met anyone that looked like me. We were both fascinated to learn about each other's childhoods. Our father was adventurous, so she grew up hiking, camping, and using air mattresses as boats in the ocean. It sounded fantastic! My heart sank thinking of all the adventures I'd missed. It wasn't all rainbows and roses, though. She grew up in the Kingdom Halls of Jehovah's Witnesses and never celebrated birthdays or holidays. Before I left our reunion, Mary told me to be careful with Roark. He molested her when she was a little girl for years. It was shocking to hear and shattered a lot of the image I'd started to build of my lost family. I didn't want to believe her. It had to be something else. She must have been remembering wrong. I ignored the information and continued on to meet our father and my three younger siblings.

Roark was married to his fourth wife and had three children together. Two boys, and the youngest was a girl. He grew up with an alcoholic mother. He said she went through partners like a deck of cards in a jailhouse common room. His resulting childhood was rife with abuse in all forms: sexual, physical, mental, and emotional. Mental health treatment was never a consideration. The only place he could think to find some relief was in a Kingdom Hall of Jehovah's Witnesses. He told me all of this over the few weeks I spent with him that summer. I could see how he became a functional alcoholic, chronic cheater, and incestuous child molester. I think he found some redemption with my 3 younger siblings, though I still pray for my youngest sister, Lilly. Given our father's history with my oldest sister and what he tried to initiate next with me, I hope she doesn't have to experience any sort of abuse.

The euphoric novelty of meeting a father I'd fantasized about my whole life came to a sudden halt my last night at his house. He was charming, handsome, and talented. He'd spent years working in construction and building their house with his wife's help. I thought all of this was impressive.

He wanted me too much. After a night of drinking, he came to my bedroom, intending to have his way with me. He was unsuccessful, and I raised hell. Not long after I left the next day, his wife took the kids and filed for divorce. Back in Southern California, I stayed drunk for an entire month, during which time I engaged in another sector of the adult entertainment industry. I wanted to die.

If death wasn't an option, I wanted to disappear. A cabin in the middle of the woods somewhere remote would do. Without hesitation, I accepted a proposal of marriage from a guy I barely knew and retreated from my party lifestyle.

~ 3 ~

SURRENDER COMES FIRST

My story should encourage others facing their trauma. It shows that anyone can heal after inhabiting a very dark place, maybe even hell. People walk out of hell and into heaven all the time—especially these days.

It seems like a wave of healing is moving throughout the globe; we're living amid rising polarity in society, politics, and economics. The strain is causing many to build resilience and grow in ways they never have before. Our mass connection builds each day and the power we cultivate increases. I'm so grateful to be alive in this time over any other.

With enormous gratitude, I recognize the person I am now is far from who I used to be. My life turned into a series of miracles once I took the first step toward healing. Surrender.

It was July 2019. I was standing in the parking lot of the health department, waiting for my ex-husband to pull up and take me back to my apartment. I'd only known James for a month before standing at the altar with him at the Chapel of the Bells in Las Vegas to say our marriage vows. We were two lost souls, but it was good we had each other back then. I met him at a Greyhound station in Los Angeles in the middle of the night, right after I'd jumped out of the window of an adult movie producer's house with my duffle bag. It was one of many strange situations I found myself in as a young woman. James had trauma from the Marines and as a government contractor afterward. It came out violently towards me when he felt like he was losing control, which was often. My traumas had birthed a modern-day gypsy, a free spirit wandering through life like La Belle Dame Sans Merci.

A silver F-250 pulled up, and I fell silent as I climbed into the passenger seat.

"So, are you pregnant?" asked James.

I kept my poker face on and stared into the distance, carefully choosing my words.

"I have a cyst. It'll go away soon, no big deal," I responded.

I didn't want to talk. Lighting a cigarette, I rolled down my window. I didn't smoke in my car, but James did in his, so I contributed to the filth. Least I could do.

He dropped me off, and I made it clear I had things to do so he wouldn't stay. James was always looking for a way back into my life. The fact that I divorced him many years prior didn't seem to sink in. Unlocking my front door, I sat down and walked over to the couch. In a daze, I recognized the hell of my own creation once again. A few weeks before this, I'd been in jail for several days. My life was a mess. Leaving Atlanta, saying goodbye to a man I loved, and generally not getting my way had pushed me to the edge of insanity. My most recent psychiatrist labeled me with depressive bipolar disorder. She prescribed me Paxil and Zyprexa to treat the symptoms of depression and psychosis. I accepted her treatment plan and diagnosis.

I did experience a few good years of calm leading up to, and immediately after, the birth of my daughter in 2013. The day she was born was a miracle. When I looked at her for the first time, I saw a clear light appear everywhere around us. Reality seemed like a dream I was waking up from, and for the first time in my life, I felt pure love. My heart opened, and I experienced inexplicable bliss. She was the first person I completely opened my heart to.

It was blatantly obvious to me after her birth that staying with her father wouldn't be possible long term. I didn't want to teach her it was okay to submit to an angry man out of fear. We moved to Georgia when she was only 1, and a year later, I filed for divorce. During the next few years, her father and I battled in court, after which time he was granted primary custody and moved with her to the Southern part of the state to be close to his family. He had been granted final decision-making over her education, which allowed him to enroll her in any school in the state. Naturally, I moved as well.

Though I had moved several hours away to be close to her, I was still running—restless, irritable, and discontent. I was in Savannah with a girlfriend and my daughter during a weekend away. We went to dinner, where I took both my doctor-prescribed medications with a few glasses of wine. My friend drove us back to where we were staying, and I blacked out in the passenger seat during the drive. The combination of pharmaceutical drugs and wine made me completely delirious and unaware of my surroundings. My daughter was in the car. While I was unconscious, she woke up and didn't recognize her surroundings. She went to the neighbors in a panic. The police were called and promptly arrested me. I regained consciousness in jail.

Sitting in the living room of my modest apartment, I could feel the cliff's edge I was teetering over. I would fall into the abyss with one more shaky step in the wrong direction. That was not an option, not now. I couldn't let my selfish desires drive me anymore. Ironically, God had given me another opportunity to correct the course of my life. I was pregnant. Again. I prepared for the only way forward. Get a regular job and blend in—absolutely no mind-altering substances of any kind, especially not pharmaceutical drugs that turn me into a zombie. In my humble opinion, no one can parent a child on such substances. At least, I couldn't. I resolved to put one foot in front of the other and live one day at a time. My knees hit the floor, and I prayed.

"God, I'm done. I'm powerless over everything. I've made a mess. I give up. You can do better than this. So, I surrender. Take my life, desires, and everything I've ever wanted. All my goals, dreams, everything. You can have it all. Do with me what you will. I choose to trust you. Amen."

Though I couldn't tell you exactly what happened at that moment, I know it was something big. It was one of the most important decisions I'd ever made in my heart. I didn't know at the time how beautiful my life would become. I had taken the first step out of hell. I always struggled with the need to be praised by others. My ego ran rampant. At that moment in my living room in 2019, I let it go. Life stabilized after falling into a rhythm of attending recovery meetings, working with a sponsor, and showing up for regular work. I cut off all communication with anybody associated with my past lifestyle. Immersed in my new life, I existed one day at a time, taking full responsibility for every word I spoke and action I took.

I had to clean up the mess with my daughter and the events that took place on the last night I ingested pharmaceutical drugs and alcohol. I was out on bail, and it would be two years before I went back to court. In hindsight, this was a blessing. I needed at least that long to calm down. The threat of losing freedom is a powerful thing. I stayed close to my little apartment in a stable routine, and slowly, things got better. Cleaning up the wreckage of my life by accepting and owning each poor decision I had made, peace entered my heart. By the end of the year, I had gained some mental clarity.

This chapter of my life reminds me of the writings of Rumi, the Sufi mystic. He said, "Knock, And He'll open the door. Vanish, And He'll make you shine like the sun. Fall, And He'll raise you to the heavens. Become nothing, And He'll turn you into everything." I didn't want to surrender until I had no other choice. It turned out that my greatest fears, once released, gave way to the greatest blessings. My ego drove my desire for external approval. Once I gave that up with humility, everything I needed came into my life synchronistically. There are priceless relationships and situations in my life today that I didn't realize were possible. 2019 was the year I fell into surrender and out of hell. Not of my own volition; grace carried me from the moment I let go.

~ 4 ~

DISCOVERING PSILOCYBIN

The first time I held my son, I threw up. I was purging all the fear I had been carrying that I could no longer afford to hold. It felt like my heart had released heavy amounts of toxins. The moment was sobering, but the worst was over, and I could gradually crescendo into the joy coming. Timothy's birth marked a new era without fear.

Having children was never something I wanted. Adoption was always of interest, but not bringing new life into existence. I couldn't bear to see someone else suffer because of what I carried. Traumas left unhealed affect family and friends. I've done lots of healing, but there's still more: generations of hurt that I've taken upon myself to alchemize. That's why I'm here. I heal myself, love my children, and dedicate my life to creating a better future. Few choose this path. It's not easy to face your biggest fears and deepest pain head-on. But I have to do it so the fear and pain don't run me or my life. I didn't plan to have children, but they're a gift. Having them motivated me to seek wholeness. Without them, I could have easily chosen to self-destruct.

After the birth of my son, caring for two beautiful children was a lot, but I managed with a sober mind. I made apologies and mended relationships as each member of my family came out to meet the newest member. Another purge came out in sobs when I expressed my regret to my sister for allowing her to watch me drag myself through utter filth for years as she watched in horror. Sometimes, people shy away from tears and sorrow. I think we should embrace moments of powerful healing. They are the catalyst for dismantling unhealthy patterns. Breaking these dysfunctional ways of being has enabled me to live a life I couldn't have imagined in darker times.

With a new baby, I completely immersed myself in work, my children, and my community. Carefully watching my words and actions, I immediately rectified any mistakes as they arose. I had gratitude, prayed daily, got enough exercise, and made a conscious effort to stay in connection with something more powerful than myself. There were plenty of people in my life to love, and I was happy. Feeling centered, I ventured back into the world of dating. The process resulted in an important connection. I spent time with someone who seemed to be on the same spiritual trajectory as me and was the catalyst for the next phase of my journey. He introduced me to the healing power of psilocybin.

This was right around the time the documentary "Fantastic Fungi" came out. In the film, mycologists explore how mycelial networks can support life in so many ways. Mushrooms are the digestive tracts of the forest. Their roots, or mycelium, enable ecosystem communication between plants. Carbon fuels the microbial community, and fungi stabilize the carbon in soils, playing an important role in ecosystem maintenance.

When ingested, the mycelial network that cultivates mushrooms has a fascinating effect on the human brain. "Fantastic Fungi" describes the effects of psilocybin, such as blending sensory experiences. Once ingesting psilocybin, people report sensations like hearing colors or seeing sounds. This is known as neuronal avalanching. The resulting changes in perception and decreased network activity in the default mode network (where the ego is developed) often cause people to experience profound growth. A person treated with psilocybin has increased brain connectivity, activating receptors. This synchronization leads to new insights, ego dissolution, and pathology disruption. Repairing places of disconnection in a neural network caused by trauma. This facilitates the right mental environment for healing.[4] Fifteen minutes into the documentary, I was sold. This led me to start down a path of accelerated healing.

I arranged to have the experience in a legal, safe, and clinical setting for psilocybin treatment. The night before my first healing ceremony, I got plenty of rest and woke up refreshed. It's best not to eat any breakfast before, so I prepared and wrote my intention for the session instead. I knew it would be important to have a destination, so the prayer I wrote echoed the growth I wanted to achieve. Human observation and focus are powerful phenomena. I came to know this on an experiential level. Directing my focus intentionally produced amazing results.

In the room set aside for the journey, I sat and sipped tea with my guide while he explained what to expect. I told him what I hoped to accomplish. He asked if I wanted to experience ego death, and I eagerly accepted the challenge. With my prayer in hand, I ate the magic medicine, and we watched some Akiane Kramarik videos on YouTube to set the tone. My favorite is "The Light," which we watched a few times. It's a beautiful depiction of the painting accompanied by her poetry set over ethereal music. The art portrays a message about the narrow path that leads to the light, which is illuminating, expansive, and transcends time.

About halfway through the third viewing of the film, I started laughing hysterically. The medicine was taking effect. The onset of laughter was like sudden altitude sickness, quick and jarring. I looked around when I calmed down. The fabric of reality had melted into a wave of beautiful, living vibrations. Astonished, I looked at my guide, who welcomed me to this new place. His face was in a state of constant fractal change, like a holographic mask. When I told him what I saw, he calmly stated he had to wear many faces. I wondered if we all have changing faces and closed my eyes to look within.

Approaching a corner of my subconscious mind, I moved into a black cloud of existence to battle self. This is a key moment that some have termed "the black mirror." I stood face to face, eyes closed, at the precipice of my worst traumas and fears. Without hesitating, I dove straight into the pool of all the painful memories of my past and became the culmination of those moments. As a child, I cried and uttered three words as I looked at my guide, "It was horrible."

He affirmed the moment and gently urged me to master the feeling and make a choice. Keep it, move it, or let it go. In a moment outside of time, I collected the old pain and pushed it out of existence, watching it dissipate into nothingness. I was free. Weightless, I opened my eyes and began a discussion with my guide about the discoveries I was experiencing. As the veil dropped, I awakened. This was the second time I'd experienced this state of consciousness. The first time was 7 years prior, when my daughter was born. In that setting, I could identify the experience as a spiritual awakening, a state brought on by the essence of love. In these moments, everything makes perfect sense, and a feeling deeper than gratitude and further than peace lights up your every cell.

In this state, I laughed at the petty grievances I'd allowed to occupy my mind only the day before. Of course, people acted ridiculously. They didn't know any better. They were sleeping. Pieces of scripture came to mind, "Then Jesus said, 'Father, forgive them; for they do not know what they are doing." As we spoke, I asked about all kinds of things: who else knew about this place? What did my guide believe? Where were we? We had a satisfying conversation about all the problems of the universe, and I left the ceremony a much healthier version of myself.

In my experience, the lessons of the medicine keep coming for a few days after a journey. The first lesson I got was about balance. An inner urge encouraged me to eat differently, exercise more effectively, and rest when needed. Psilocybin can wake up my biological intuition; it tells me what I need. Of course, it's common knowledge that living a balanced life catalyzes health and well-being. However, knowing this on a cellular level is where transformation occurs. My desire to consume knowledge about mental, biological, and spiritual wellness became insatiable.

~ 5 ~

EAT FROM THE TREE OF LIFE

Having used psilocybin as an aid in therapeutic treatments a few times, I've noticed certain patterns. I can hear sounds and see matter that is not normally within my realm of perception. This is called neural avalanching[5]. The sounds I hear while listening to meditation music during a therapy session seem to be in higher frequencies, which I didn't notice before. It's as if those sounds allow my brain waves to vibrate at a higher frequency, picking up bits of information on that level.

NeuroHealth explains how they measure and classify the frequencies of brain waves in neuroscience.

"The EEG (electroencephalograph) measures brainwaves of different frequencies within the brain. Electrodes are placed on specific sites on the scalp to detect and record the electrical impulses within the brain. A frequency is the number of times a wave repeats itself within a second. You can compare it to tuning into frequencies on a radio. Researchers usually describe the raw EEG in terms of frequency bands: Gamma greater than 30 (Hz), BETA (13-30Hz), ALPHA (8-12 Hz), THETA (4-8 Hz), and

DELTA (less than 4 Hz). Our brain uses 13Hz (high alpha or low beta) for "active" intelligence. Often, we find individuals who exhibit learning disabilities and attention problems having a deficiency of 13Hz activity in certain brain regions that affects the ability to perform sequencing tasks and math calculations easily."[6]

Tools like a tonoscope can observe the vibrational aspect of a frequency, and each unique frequency carries with it a specific geometrical pattern. The study of repeating wave patterns through a medium such as water is called cymatics[7], derived from the Greek word for "wave." It's possible a living organism operating from a brain frequency band above Alpha could also visibly observe frequency vibrations.

In this higher state of awareness brought on by psilocybin, I can see the vibratory nature of physical matter around me. Not only do solid objects appear more fluid and alive, but the usually empty space between solid objects also transforms into a series of patterns. The shapes form geometric mandalas, always revealing the existence of vibrations everywhere. When I looked up the root meaning of the word "hallucinate," I learned it comes from the Greek *alyein* or *halyein*, which means to "wander in mind." Wandering, exploring, and discovering should be encouraged!

In a recent psilocybin-assisted therapy session, I saw the familiar mandala patterns as the surrounding wood danced and the words I had written came alive. This time, I had a close friend with me who was more advanced at seeing through our holographic world. She lit some palo santo and rang a sound bowl, hitting perfect "C" notes. Sitting with me, Lauren pointed out a specific pattern within the geometrical shapes around us we could both see—the flower of life.

As I explore the deepest parts of my psyche and the surrounding world in these moments, I notice abilities that stem from a deeper connection. When I was aware of the flower of life pattern, I closed my eyes and knelt in a yogic child's pose. I was in a garden in the midst of creation.

I can't geographically locate the transcendent place, but people I've spoken with since say they can reach it in meditation. I embodied a beautiful light, like a star. Feeling the light and color all around me, pink and gold flooded my senses. Reducing these moments into words is difficult. Especially in English, since we *spell* our words. Other languages **build** their words.

In the Indian yoga tradition, *sahaja samadhi* is a concept that mirrors the Gnostic teachings of Jesus. The attainment of bliss effortlessly reached from a meditative state of "being" rather than "doing" establishes a connection with a person's higher self. The clarity received from this place of mental calm provides a person with profound insights. Yogis believe the higher self is the divine aspect of all beings and can be reached through a higher state of consciousness known as *samadhi*.

After spending some time experiencing *samadhi*, I sat up straight back and looked around the garden. Lauren was sitting facing me, bathed in purple light like a magical fairy. To my pleasant surprise, she looked the same as she normally does, just more herself and timeless. I realized while I was taking in my surroundings where we were. I looked at Lauren with wonder and confirmed by asking, "The Garden of Eden?" She smiled and nodded, remembering herself. The flower of life was all around us. With understanding on a telepathic level, we acknowledged each other and expressed deep gratitude for the reconnection.

The Flower of Life

8

Before this experience, I had read about the study of frequencies. I knew that musical notes have vibratory signatures that form patterns when measured in sand or water. Since Lauren had made a perfect "C" note with the sound bowl before we saw the flower of life, I had to find out the vibratory signature of a "C" note within cymatics. The Flower of Life is pictured above.

Meinl Sonic Energy is a company dedicated to providing instruments for use in sound therapy with the help of sound specialists around the world. Their research into the "C" note led them to findings from Rudolf Steiner and Guiseppe Verdi.

"This note was described as being the central tone of creation by the legendary philosopher Rudolf Steiner and the famous Italian composer Guiseppe Verdi. The tone C at 128 hertz can be looked upon as the tone of the center of ultimate balance." Somehow, Lauren and I had both reached balance, allowing us to see the center of creation in the geometry around us. Perhaps where we went together could be described as a state of mind.

Have you ever noticed that when a particular topic stands out for you, you come across it more often? The day after that psilocybin ceremony, I was listening to the Psychedelic Assisted Therapy Global Summit. One speaker mentioned the Garden of Eden at the end of his talk, suggesting his hope for humanity in the next couple of decades is to enter the garden together. I don't believe in coincidences anymore. Since this experience, I've heard more people discussing the Garden. The Hebrew word Eden literally means bliss. It's a state of being.

Aubrey Marcus, one of my favorite podcast hosts, made the most eloquent depiction of this discovery in his spoken word poetry, "Welcome to the Garden." I can't imagine another time in which I would rather be alive. The truth that unfolds in my heart with each experience is indescribable. Everything is full of meaning, and no depth is too far.

Scholars Harsha Kuriakose and Eric Soreng, Ph. D. of the University of Delhi, explore the Garden of Eden as it relates to the human psyche in *The Garden of Eden: Creation and Consciousness.*

"The Garden of Eden mentioned in the sacred narrative is not an ordinary garden but a utopian paradisal one like the Greek Garden of Hesperides, the Western paradise of Buddhism, the

Elysian Fields, etc. This paradisal garden "is the imagined locus of our beginning and end, the original matrix and mandala of life, fed by underground sources of living waters" (Ronnberg, 2010, p. 146). For the faithful always yearns to return to this original condition of being in a state of oneness with God in his divine care and protection as it was in the beginning before the fall. In the Book of Revelation, St John describes the heavenly vision of the restoration of Eden and a call to partake in the tree of life whose leaves are supposed to be the "cure for the nations" (Revelation 22: 1-2; Ezekiel 47: 12)."[9]

The spiritual masters echoed throughout humanity's ancient texts pointed the way to restore our connection to source. People have referred to "Source" as Prana, Chi, and scalar energy, to name a few. Could the presence of the flower of life indicate the restoration of this connection? Many ancient archeological sites around the world depict the flower of life. For instance, in the Temple of Osiris in Abydos, Egypt. The Forbidden City in Beijing, China. There is even a depiction on the side of a 19th-century shed near my home in southern Georgia. Almost like a portal marking, follow the flower to find the Garden in which the Tree of Life grows in abundance. Having seen the flower of life before recognizing the Garden of Eden, I had to look deeper into the story of the Tree of Life.

Britannica defines the Tree of Life as "the source of life, a force that connects all lives, or the cycle of life and death itself."[10] There's a brainwave frequency that corresponds with a state of bliss. Eden means bliss. I have come to believe through my experiences that humanity being "kicked out of the Garden of Eden" was simply a lowering of consciousness into a state of duality. A lower vibration of brainwaves. Accessing this state of awareness allows a person to experience Eden or Nirvana, and different cultures have described it in different ways. The bible and kabbalah talk about the Tree of Life, and now science has discovered the pattern of the flower of life appearing when a C note is made. Genesis 2:9 in the bible states, "The Tree of Life was in the midst of the garden." In Hebrew, the word tree (Etz) is built (not *spelled*) with two letters: Ayin and Tzadik. The translation of ayin is "eye," and the translation of tzadik is "righteous one." The Tree of Life in Hebrew is called *etz hayyim. Hayyim* can mean living, life, or alive. Breaking the Hebrew down this way, the translation of Genesis 2:9 would read, "The eye of the righteous one is alive in the midst of the garden." Looking at this Hebrew translation, it seems that the "eye" the text is talking about is more like the third eye, the eye of perception, rather than our two physical eyes. Being in a harmonizing state of existence with love allows for the eye of awareness to open. Thus, there is a way to transcend our current level of perception and enter the garden. Eat from the Tree of Life.

I am grateful for the journey of this lifetime and amazed at the opportunities it presents. Yes, there are horrors. I've lived many. However, I choose to direct my focus on the illuminating light of truth in love. I believe some people are walking around in hell, and others in heaven. When I lived in isolation, the reality I existed in was hell. Living in connection with myself and others allows for synchronistic glimpses into a world that is better than anything I could imagine alone. We are constantly creating the projection of reality from within ourselves through our awareness. I believe eternity is right now, just outside of space and time. There is no waiting for someone to come, save us, and take us there. We make the moment. I am, and I create out of a place of connection with the energy of love. Energy is emotion in motion. Love is the currency of the universe. A frequency available to those who seek it out.

On a global scale, people from all professional backgrounds and cultures are stepping into their power. Using their stories and unique perspectives, they're moving past the fear of controversy in pursuit of truth. Every day, more of us find our voices to communicate insights with a common goal of healing humanity.

Every ancient text found on the planet alludes to awakening. Breaking down the barriers of my life experiences allowed me to access a new perspective. I'm not a doctor, scientist, lawyer, or any other notable professional. I am a single mom, raising two children in a rural town, far removed from my past. As I continue to grow, this is the lens I present to the collective to cultivate inspiration and encouragement for others trying to remember.

~ 6 ~

HEALING THE MIND

POSITIVE SELF-TALK

I'd already started working towards healing before I made the intentional choice to stop ingesting harmful substances. They dulled my thoughts and emotions. A colleague gave me a book about the power of my thoughts, about directing your thoughts positively, especially thoughts toward oneself. The information given in the book was an important piece of the puzzle of self-healing that I was tackling. Seeds were planted. It took a total shift in mentality and discovering my power to uncover the essence of truth that I now passionately pursue.

When I was numbing my mind using drugs and alcohol and things prescribed by a doctor, my thoughts were detrimental to my well-being. They stemmed from a belief from a very young age that I wasn't important. Comparing myself to others was an ongoing habit. It caused me to see lack everywhere and cultivate resentments based on envy. When I chose to engage in that way of thinking, what I ingested contributed to my self-destruction. When my thoughts are consciously productive, I ingest helpful things that contribute to my overall well-being. I'm the creator of my reality. My thoughts direct my words, which direct my actions. This is how I started to heal my mind. I shifted my thinking when I realized how damaging my self-talk was, but it didn't happen overnight. It was a couple of years before I could settle into a rhythm of positive self-talk.

Positive thinking can feel like a superpower at first. Suddenly, if I had a negative thought, I didn't have to accept it. Thoughts that didn't sit well with me got reworded to be more helpful—a simple concept, sure, but with a profound impact. When I changed my thoughts and words, the new habits I adopted transformed my behavior. This is the gradual progression that moved me away from choosing exploitation. If I chose to believe everything is important, including myself, self-love became an essential element of my new beliefs.

There are still times when someone suggests I rent out my body. Being a single mother living in a very low-income area of the country with little opportunity has narrowed my options for obtaining financial stability. It's still a struggle. Some people who don't understand the spiritual and emotional damage that engaging in a lifestyle of prostitution presents wonder why I don't pursue what they view as easy money. 16 years after being trafficked, such a proposition isn't a consideration. I've lived the repercussions and wouldn't trade the healing I've found for a shortcut. Working hard consistently towards my goals has gotten me much further in the long run than drugs, alcohol, and prostitution ever did. It may take longer, but it's definitely worth it.

Along the way, I learned other techniques to accompany this new practice of positive self-talk. For instance, I learned

EFT, which stands for "emotional freedom technique," and TFT, "thought field therapy." I would think about a problem and create a positive statement about the situation to repeat out loud. For instance, if I was having trouble finding my voice and communicating clearly with a problematic employee at work, I could use a statement to reinforce positive self-talk around that situation. Using this example, I might say, "I, Sarah, am loving, compassionate, and understanding. People I interact with feel accepted, creating relational harmony that allows for productive communication". I would tap my Meridian points on my body while repeating that statement a few times a day for as long as it took for the situation to resolve itself.

What are meridian points? The National Library of Medicine defines them as strings connecting acupuncture points, which are considered passageways through which energy flows throughout the body in traditional Chinese medicine[11]. The meridian system is composed of 12 principal meridians, each of which connects to an organ system and extends to an extremity and eight collaterals. EFT and TFT facilitated a change in perspective when I needed to break through old thinking patterns. Learning new tools and using them to develop healthy habits is invaluable.

EDUCATION

Consuming large amounts of information about health, well-being, and spirituality was initially frightening. I had grown up believing that the pursuit of knowledge is evil. Part of this was religious conditioning about being careful with what I read. Having been raised in fundamentalist Christianity, I had to stick with the Protestant Bible as the only truth about God. No one commanded me to think this way. It's what I understood to be the point of what I was learning in church, based on the teachings of the Protestant bible. For years, I wanted to read spiritual texts apart from the Bible. To expand my awareness. My hesitance in doing so was because of a belief I had formed that I would be damned to hell if I did. When I read other texts, starting with the Book of Enoch, I realized there is truth everywhere when you look for it. What I focus on grows. If I am focused on validating my fear, I will find it. If I focus on discovering the truth, I will find it.

In Anna Lembke's book *Dopamine Nation*, she talks about the effect learning has on the release of dopamine in the brain.

"Learning increases dopamine firing in the brain. Female rats housed for three months in a diverse, novel, and stimulating environment show a proliferation of dopamine-rich synapses in the brain's reward pathway compared to rats housed in standard laboratory cages. The brain changes that occur in response to a stimulating and novel environment are similar to those seen with high-dopamine (addictive) drugs."[12]

Finding a balance between pursuing knowledge and grounding new information can be challenging. I've found it helpful to take breaks between learning new information to practice what I learned before I explore something else. For example, I had an epiphany about how to make my son feel loved. I watched how his face lit up when I sat down to play Hot Wheels with him or the look of hope in his eyes when he asked if I would color with him. If I had kept doing what I was doing before, I might have missed an opportunity to nurture him and grow as a mom. Learning through observation allowed me to see an opportunity to expand on the love he feels from me by spending quality time with him, strengthening our connection. If I hadn't paused to spend time with him, implementing what I learned, I might have skipped over an important opportunity.

PLANT MEDICINE

Incorporating plant medicine to speed up the healing I had already chosen has proven invaluable. My perceptions have transformed by participating in legal healing ceremonies with clinical controls. Again, none of this information should be taken as more than a personal experience under those conditions.

Any medicine I put in my body develops a kind of symbiotic relationship between the medicine and my body. Psilocybin allows me to intuitively discover what my mind, body, and spirit connection need to regain equilibrium. It grabs my attention and shows me exactly what needs to be addressed and how. Over time, I'm able to resolve issues as they arise more easily, having integrated the process of healing using psilocybin as a tool.

The way mushrooms grow mirrors how I imagine they assist in the healing of neural pathways in my brain. Mushrooms are the fruit of a mycelial network that spreads underground, like a computer network. It spreads for miles, connecting plants and trees and even working as a communication system in certain circumstances.

Paul Stamets is an American mycologist and entrepreneur who advocates for the use of medicinal fungi. He often discusses the benefits of the mycelial network extending 300 miles down into the earth. In his book *Mycelium Running: How Mushrooms Can Help Save the World*, he said,

"I believe mycelium is the neurological network of nature. Interlacing mosaics of mycelium infuse habitats with information-sharing membranes. These membranes are aware, react to change, and collectively have the long-term health of the host environment in mind. The mycelium stays in constant molecular communication with its environment, devising diverse enzymatic and chemical responses to complex challenges."

What could be a more complex challenge for an individual than the effect trauma has on their brain development? Thinking about how mushrooms fruit from this mycelial network, it makes sense that each session results in feelings of connection within myself and the surrounding world.

When the medicine takes effect, I gain compelling urges to engage in whatever my body needs. For instance, if I have been going for weeks at a time without enough sleep, I can feel my body immediately relax and get heavy—a biological prompting to rest. There have been times when I needed to process trauma, and the psilocybin brought to the forefront of my mind the memories associated with it for me to work through and heal. It's like kneading a knotted muscle on an emotional level. I'm able to take on that experience and think it through in a way that brings enlightenment and closure. Psilocybin allows neural connections to fire synapses in different areas of the brain. Once psilocybin is introduced, the brain lights up like a Christmas tree. I feel those effects by what I am prompted to take on during a session, and I always walk away feeling improved. Before going on one of these healing journeys, I always experience psychological resistance. After taking it, the fear dissipates, even if I spend an hour working through memories that I would have otherwise tried to avoid resolving.

This experience reinforces my belief in the healing benefits of psilocybin, without concern about some of the serious side effects found in pharmaceutical drugs, like antidepressants. On December 1st, 2022, Dr. Caroline MacCallum of the University of British Columbia published the article *Therapeutic use of psilocybin: Practical considerations for dosing and administration* in Frontiers in Psychiatry:

"Due to psilocybin's large therapeutic index (1:1000) and a typically unattainable lethal dose, psilocybin has a favorable safety profile. Relative to other psychedelics (such as MDMA, DMT, etc.), psilocybin has a lower occurrence of seizures, hospital admissions, and other serious adverse effects and lacks addictive or reinforcing properties. Several dose-escalating studies have tested the subjective psychedelic effects in supratherapeutic doses, e.g., 50–60 mg or 5–6 grams, and found positive results with little-to-no safety concerns."[13]

SELF-HEALING ALCHEMY

Using psilocybin, I organically developed a self-healing technique to clear past trauma brought to light. Diving head-first into lingering pain without fear allows for transmutation.

During a session, I remembered my younger self at three years old. Sitting on a bed in a hotel room holding a baby doll, baby food, and a bottle. I was afraid and alone. Going back in time to that moment in meditation, I sat with my 3-year-old self. I held the little girl and told her how beautiful, important, supported, and loved she was. I told her she had everything she needed, and help was on the way. Even when she felt alone, she wasn't. This was a suppressed memory I had of neglect. My birth mother had left me in a room for days.

The technique was deeply healing. Being outside the moment but inside the memory allowed me to notice an important detail. I was giving the baby doll I held the care I craved—everything I needed. Thankfully, as an adult, I have all those things. I could go back in time and give my 3-year-old self what she gave the doll —love, support, understanding, nourishment, and rest. What's even more incredible about this memory is the name I picked for the baby doll. It was a girl, but I named her Timothy. Thirty years later, that's what I named my son. The name Timothy represents freedom from fear. When I was pregnant with him, I read a verse in 2 Timothy of the Bible. It says, "For God has not given us a spirit of fear but of power and love and a sound mind." The birth of my son represented freedom from fear.

Overall, early childhood neglect can have a wide range of detrimental impacts on brain development, affecting many different cognitive, emotional, and social functioning elements.[14] These consequences can last throughout adulthood and contribute to a variety of mental health issues. My anxiety, depression, and attachment disorder resulted from the impact of early childhood trauma.

Attachment disorders are common, with inconsistencies in early attachment relationships between a child and their primary caregiver. I identify with having experienced Reactive Attachment Disorder (RAD), which results in avoiding physical contact. Even as an adult, I'm reluctant to hug most people. Growing up, my lack of emotional regulation was due to an interruption in neural connectivity. These neural pathways are important for coping with stress and other overwhelming emotions. I couldn't handle small stresses for much of my life, crying over spilled milk, quite literally. Engaging in relationships was difficult because of the depth of emotion that kind of connection brings. Romantic relationships were nearly impossible. My belief that I was unimportant and undeserving of having what I craved motivated me to run from the people I wanted most. Therefore, I chose partners that I had less feelings for. Being around people was easier if I didn't feel a deep sense of connection. Poor choice of partners could merely be a byproduct of damage to my prefrontal cortex because of the neglect present during the first five years of life!

Remembering I am enough despite my early experiences has been an important step in my healing journey. To know oneself is imperative for growth. Many people live their whole lives never discovering who they are and why they're here. As someone who was adopted, I felt I didn't quite fit in. This belief created separation.

I wondered where my birth parents were almost constantly throughout my childhood. Did they ever love me? Did they forget I existed? Questions went through my mind about whether or not they valued me. Later in life, I came to understand it didn't matter what led them to abandon me. My world took care of me and always would. My value doesn't depend on the people who brought me into this world or their thoughts towards me. They are broken. I carry deep gratitude for the opportunity to be nurtured and grow amongst people who truly knew how to love and taught me the same. I understand many adopted people share similar struggles. To heal, I had to go from believing I'm enough to knowing for sure.

An interesting correlation between knowledge and lack of education is key to my healing. When I took substances I knew nothing about, the effect was destructive mentally, emotionally, spiritually, and physically. However, when my mentality shifted from a scarcity mindset to an abundant outlook, I realized everything has importance. I've often heard a saying that goes something like, either God is everything, or he is nothing. That tells me either everything is deeply significant or nothing is. In paying attention, I noted what exactly I was putting into my body. This informed approach has allowed me to take responsibility for my health. What started as an intuitive biological prompt to consume the right things turned into a discovery of the inner workings of my body that is essential to the time I'm living in.

MEDITATION

Uncovering the realization that I am the creator of my reality has paved the way for an ongoing transformation. Applying techniques such as mindfulness in meditation has allowed me to create a life of joy. In his author's manuscript on *Employing Pain and Mindfulness to Understand Consciousness*, Joshua Grant finds, "While much could be said concerning the definition of mindfulness, for present purposes, we consider mindfulness as a form of non-reactive awareness of one's present-moment experience. Mindfulness can be considered a meta-cognitive state that exists to varying degrees in everyone. It can also be trained and developed by mindfulness-based practices".[15] To perceive the moment without reacting to it is how I've been able to transcend many negative emotions, especially in the last couple of years.

Creating balance in every aspect of my life has been a persistent theme as I continue to move beyond exploitation. I research everything I put into my body and move through exercises with more confidence and flow. Every choice I make is conscious, from fulfilling work I take on to relationships I cultivate. It's essential to practice self-care and protect my energy from manipulative people. This allows for rapid growth. It's not unlike how a plant needs sunlight, water, and nutrients to thrive and grow. I believe in harmonic thought, loving interaction, and deliberate action as building blocks for the person I choose to become. These three foundational aspects of my makeup are mental, spiritual, and physical.

RESONANCE

It's not enough to heal the mind. Yet, as I move away from exploitation, the neurological workings of the mind lead me naturally to look at the physical elements of the brain. Brain waves vibrate at rates that interact with frequencies in the environment. Scientists measure the brain's waves in bands ranging from gamma to delta. In 2019, the Institute of Physics published an article titled, *Innovative technical implementation of the Schumann resonances and its influence on organisms and biological cells.* The author cites Tesla:

"Alpha waves in the human brain are between 6 and 8 hertz. The wave frequency of the human cavity resonates between 6 and 8 hertz. All biological systems operate in the same frequency range. The human brain's alpha waves function in this range, and the electrical resonance of the earth is between 6 and 8 hertz. Thus, our entire biological system – the brain and the earth–work on the same frequencies. If we can control that resonate system electronically, we can directly control the entire mental system of humankind".

An alpha Theta brainwave frequency in the human brain vibrates at 7.83 hertz. This is the same frequency that the Earth vibrates at as well, known as the Schumann resonance[16].

Our brain waves function like antennae, tuning into the spectrum of frequencies in our environment. Sonya Joseph of the American College of Healthcare Sciences concluded in her 2019 thesis, "Tuning into specific frequencies can assist with combating man-made Electromagnetic Frequencies that cause disease, disharmony, and amplifying negativity." Certain sounds, such as rain or a middle C note, vibrating between 174 Hertz and 963 Hertz positively impact our mental, physical, and spiritual health.[17]

When I think about music, I can identify certain emotions with certain songs or genres. Classical music puts me in a calm state of mind that I like to pair with writing. Each era of our history carries with it a certain sound. When I tune into a radio station, I can immediately tell if the song playing is from the '80s, '90s, 2000s, 2010s, or the current decade.

Resonance describes the impact of an outside influence on human emotion. It's also used to describe the impact of frequencies on our brain waves, which can actually be measured by science[18]. Our bodies contain 60% water, a medium commonly used to observe the patterns emitted by different frequencies. Like the ones found on the solfeggio scale in music, healing frequencies can align the ocean of our emotions and create an emotional state of peace.

As discovered by Pythagorean, each of the frequencies on this scale adds up to 3, 6, or 9. A 2014 study used sound frequencies to induce drought tolerance in rice plants. The authors state, "...sound treatment triggers drought tolerance by changing the elasticity and flexibility of the cell wall, which affects the ability of plants to absorb water".[19]

When I allowed fear to be the driving force in my life, I felt a separation within myself and in my external environment. In my healing journey, each stage progressed immediately after a release of fear. As I've healed, I can better love myself and connect with the people I love in my life. For me, fear represents separation, while love enables and represents connection.

The harmonic nature of the solfeggio frequencies positively resonates with the body, creating a magnetic alignment environment. All rhythms of life seek harmony. The way pendulums swing in sync over time shows this. Women menstruate in coordination when they are frequently around each other.

The magnetic nature of living things falling into alignment can be traced back to sound. If love was a frequency, it could heal my entire being by bringing my physical, mental, and spiritual aspects into perfect alignment. I wonder, what frequency does unconditional love vibrate at? If we could tap into this frequency, we could heal ourselves and the world—every subject of study in life points to a desire to tap into this frequency. Spirituality aims to instill love into interpersonal relationships.

I can think of several paths to take in order to tap into this frequency. Historically, religions all over the world have used different forms of meditation to connect with something greater than the physical world. The Essenes are a sect of Judaism like the Pharisees or Sadducees. Joseph and Mary, the parents of Jesus, grew up in the Essene community and practiced Samadhi. In Hinduism, a meditation derived from the Vedas (the most ancient Hindu scriptures) uses mantras visually and audibly to expand awareness. Many thought leaders in this age promote transcendental meditation to pursue a higher plane of existence. The goal is to reach a place of stillness that allows one to feel unconditional love, which carries a unique vibration.

Another path to tap into the frequency of unconditional love is with plant medicine. Psilocybin is just one of these avenues. Many ceremonies explore the expanded state of consciousness in which higher frequencies are perceivable. Ayahuasca, peyote, and tobacco are some examples. Neural coherence deals with synchronicities. Ingesting certain nootropics can enable a person to access a flow state by entering an alpha-theta brain band. For example, Nootropics Expert Founder David Tomen finds, "L-Theanine boosts alpha brain waves (8-12Hz) promoting alert relaxation. And theta brain waves are associated with creativity and relief from trauma." As the act of creating flows from this state, the universe reflects signs of encouragement, like repeated number patterns.

From the lens of my experience, moving away from separation and towards healing starts with the removal of fear and ends with the embodiment of love. Many doors open onto this path. Studying geometry, alchemy, anthropology, physics, art, and music can all help move someone closer to unconditional love. The path toward living in harmonic resonance is narrow, but it is the only path that resonates perfectly with my soul.

Existing moment by moment, I aim to move at the speed of thought, create from a state of flow, and relate with the power of love.

~ 7 ~

DISCOVERING THE "I AM"

In the short time after I began my healing journey, I now understood knowing my higher self to be an important aspect of the process. I scheduled another psilocybin ceremony to be performed in a legal and clinical setting and prepared to make this discovery. I kept the intention of meeting my higher self at the forefront of my mind as I began the session. When the medicine started taking effect, I meditated. The sensations of feeling color and tasting sound washed over me as I tried to go back to my birth, to my mother's womb, and whatever came before. I was shaking, sweating, and blocked. It felt uncomfortable, and I couldn't conjure up the memories. So, I stood up and walked over to a mirror.

The room I was in was completely dark, yet a light enveloped me. I could clearly see everything around me. Sitting cross-legged in front of the mirror, I concentrated. My holographic form stared back at me. I was ancient, yet youthful, with hair that moved like the mane of a lioness. I went back further and further, changing but still the same through what seemed like lifetimes. Then I got to the core. In the mirror, I saw myself as who I truly am, my highest self. I am. I felt this knowledge in every cell of my body as I remembered who I am.

Having found the answer to the question I brought on the journey, I laid down and listened to the meditation music playing in the background. It took on a multi-dimensional quality. I could hear sounds I hadn't heard before, like flutes at a high frequency. It felt like I was transported to a place before time, in which all of creation was harmoniously composed into existence.

As I experienced this unfolding of life all around me, a trumpet was blown like a call. I sat up and looked at my guide, and for a moment, I thought I was being taken into heaven. Jesus had come back! A wave of panic hit me as I questioned whether my friends and family were coming too. I asked my guide if my children were coming, and he assured me I wasn't going to leave them. They were being cared for and safe. I knew that, but we were on our way to *heaven*! I called out their names as well as the names of each member of my family. I was looking for them because it was time. I was ascending and didn't want to leave anyone behind. Yes, this probably sounds crazy. However, the experience helped me unpack deeper truths around the story of the second coming that I assumed I knew the meaning of. Time is a construct that has been ordered into our reality. Eternity is just outside of time in the present moment, and the feeling of being a part of the sounds of creation became a memory I got to relive.

Known as the great "I Am," Jesus is an important aspect of Western culture. To truly understand the message, I investigated the concept of "I am" from different perspectives around the world.

In a 2008 Ted Talk, Neuroscientist Jill Bolte Taylor described her near-death experience while having a stroke[20]. She recognized that the hemorrhaging in the left hemisphere of her brain allowed her to step into her right hemisphere. Her resulting experience of nirvana gave her a life-changing perspective on the nature of reality, which she has applied to her work. In her closing comments, she said,

"We are the life-force power of the Universe, with manual dexterity and two cognitive minds. And we have the power to choose, moment by moment, who and how we want to be in the world. Right here, right now, I can step into the consciousness of my right hemisphere, where we are 'I am.' The life-force power of the Universe. At one with all this, I am the life-force power of the 50 trillion beautiful molecular geniuses that make up my form."

It's hard to explain how my life underwent such a complete transformation so quickly after I surrendered my egoic will. I credit the life force power Dr. Taylor referred to in her speech. Allowing that unnamable power of the universe to create through me has given me a chance to experience life in flow. It's effortless.

THE EGO

Taking responsibility for my life, I make the choice to create my reality rather than react to it. I no longer feel like a victim of people, places, and experiences. Life is happening for me, not to me. Behind my surface desires for recognition, praise, and comfort lies a deep knowing that I already am and have everything I need. Stripping away unhelpful thoughts and fears, I can uncover this essence. It is a continual process. I believe the more we heal, the closer we are to remembering who we are and where we are. That's how we break free from inaccurate perceptions.

Many great spiritual masters and subject matter geniuses have described the disadvantages of a person driven by their ego. In his book *Be Love Now*, Ram Dass wrote[21], "As you dissolve into love, your ego fades. You're not thinking about loving; you're just being love, radiating like the sun." My ego can drive me toward addiction and destruction if I allow it to direct my choices. It has unrealistic expectations. Another philosophical writer, Alan Watts[22], said, "The ego-self constantly pushes reality away. It constructs a future out of empty expectations and a past out of regretful memories."

I can embrace joy more readily by stripping away my expectations and experiencing life as it unfolds. Before adopting this philosophy, I was constantly disappointed by people, places, and circumstances. I wanted everything and everyone in my life to mirror back to me an unconditional love I'd never known. I didn't know I had to dig it out of myself before creating it in my outer reality. I turned mostly to alcohol to numb feelings of disappointment and inadequacy, disconnecting from reality. The way I existed from blackout to blackout, I should have died. Living without dependency on mind-numbing substances, I allow myself to process the lows and highs of life. The more I put my ego to death, the more I heal.

THE "I AM" AND JESUS

It seems the more I strip away layers of ego, the more curiosity I cultivate about what lies underneath. The same insatiable search for the truth that led me to discover my biological origins continues to motivate me. In John 14:6 of King James' bible, Jesus states, "I am the way, the truth, and the light." It seems his teachings pointed to a narrow path that illuminates the underlying truth in all things. The more I realize this, the more I experience an expanded awareness of interconnectedness.

In 1945, a collection of early Christian Gnostic texts was found in caves near Nag Hammadi, Egypt. It's thought that these scriptures most closely represent the teachings of the Essene sect of Judaism. If that sounds familiar, it's because Mary and Joseph in the bible were part of the Essene religion. In one of the Nag Hammadi Scriptures, the Gospel of Thomas, a verse reads, "(77) Jesus said, "It is I who am the light which is above them all. It is I who am the All. From me did the All come forth, and unto me did the All extend. Split a piece of wood, and I am there. Lift up the stone, and you will find me there." It seems Jesus' view of reality came from a place of connection with the world around him. This sounds like Jesus is relating himself to the same life force power of the universe that Dr. Jill Taylor discussed in her speech.

Expanding on this idea of Jesus embodying all, in the Teachings of Silvanus in the Nag Hammadi, there are further insights about this concept.

"Furthermore, it is difficult to comprehend him, and it is difficult to find Christ. For he is the one who dwells in every place, and also, he is in no place. For no one who wants to will be able to know God as he actually is, nor Christ, nor the Spirit, nor the chorus of angels, nor even the archangels, as well as the thrones of the spirits, and the exalted lordships, and the Great Mind. If you do not know yourself, you will not be able to know all of these. Open the door for yourself, that you may know the One who is. Knock on yourself, that the Word may open for you. For he is the Ruler of Faith and the Sharp Sword, having become all for everyone because he wishes to have mercy on everyone."

Jesus is pointing to the importance of knowing yourself to discover higher truths.

THE "I AM" IN CULTURE

Modern neuroscience, spiritual masters, and christianity are not the only places we find this concept of the "I Am" if we look carefully. The connection to our higher selves through the cultivation of a knowing of oneself is a central theme in the Bhagavad Gita. In this Hindu text, the Supreme Lord describes himself similarly to Jesus. In chapter 9, verse 17, the Supreme Lord states, "I am the father of this universe, the mother, the support, and the grandsire. I am the object of knowledge, the purifier, and the syllable om. I am also the Rk, the Sama, and the Yajur [Vedas]." To know this I am, life force energy. Yogis practice physical, spiritual, and mental purification. Their practices seek to uncover the true essence of being.

The idea of going within to attain spiritual growth by connecting with invisible energy is also echoed in the ancient mystical texts known as the Hermetica. Hermetic writings tie together theological and philosophical ideas from both ancient Greece and Egypt. One of the prophets in these texts is known as Thoth by the Egyptians and Hermes Trismegistus by the Greeks. In the

Wisdom of the Corpus Hermetica, Hermes says, "Where could matter be placed if it existed apart from God [who is infinite]? Would it not be but a confused mass unless it were ordered? And if it is ordered, by whom is it ordered? The energies which operate in it are parts of God. Whether you speak of matter, bodies, or substance, know that all these are the energy of God, of the God who is all. In the All, there is nothing that is not God. Adore this teaching, my child, and hold it sacred." Again, the universal life force energy that is in all things is described in these lines.

Another example of this energy can be found in modern-day Iran in the fire temples of the Zoroastrians. Their one God is referred to as Ahura Mazda. The Gathas discuss "the One Life" of the world in their sacred hymns. Here are some verses that refer to this energy.

Yasna 30.9: "The life of the world comes to us through the Good Mind, the Good Word, and the Good Deed. All life is one, and we are all united in our dependence on the One Life."

Yasna 34.1: "The One Life flows through all living beings, and all are sustained by its nourishment. Let us honor the One Life and work to preserve its unity."

Yasna 44.2: "The One Life gives rise to all creation, and all creation reflects its divine nature. Let us strive to recognize the unity of all things and work to promote harmony and balance in the world."

Yasna 51.6: "The One Life is the source of all power and vitality and sustains us in our daily lives. Let us strive to live in harmony with the One Life and work to promote its growth and flourishing."

These verses portray an understanding of the essential energy at the root of all things. Zoroastrianism was the first monotheistic belief system that made its way into our current historical worldview as a collective. It seems as far back as I go in recorded history, universal life force energy is referred to. This esoteric knowledge has made its way into my inner knowing. It is what I could identify sitting in front of the mirror, searching for my higher self. I am. I am the universal life force energy that powers our universe. I am an individualized expression of this energy. When I interact with others, we mirror each other—dancing in love that is encapsulated in life force energy, like a still pond reflecting the trees above and dissolving the separation of earth and sky.

~ 8 ~

SEEING THE MATRIX

Olympic gold medalist in rowing and award-winning researcher in human performance, Jennifer Walinga, writes about human consciousness. In her textbook, *Introduction to Psychology*, she states.

"Consciousness is the awareness of the self in space and time. It can be defined as human awareness of both internal and external stimuli. Researchers study states of human consciousness and differences in perception to understand how the body works to produce conscious awareness. Consciousness varies in both arousal and content, and there are two types of conscious experience: phenomenal, or in the moment, and access, which recalls experiences from memory."[23]

It is generally agreed upon that several core elements make up the human perception of reality: consciousness, energy, information (cognition), societal conditioning, and time.

59

Consciousness also plays a role in how someone sees and interacts with the world around them. In chapter 6, "Healing the Mind," I wrote about brain waves. I believe that higher brain wave function correlates with a more expanded and accurate view of external reality. We can attain higher brain wave functions using nootropics, meditation, mindfulness, fasting, or ingesting certain herbs or plants. Our brains communicate with our bodies and cause us to feel through the sensations of sound, taste, touch, smell, and sight. These are the senses we know of, though some believe many more undiscovered senses exist. In the scientific community, this is caused by increased global integration, leading to expanded sensory perception. Our brains adapt to our environment, as shown in a 2017 study conducted by the Massachusetts Eye and Ear Infirmary:

"On the scans of those with early blindness, the team observed structural and functional connectivity changes, including evidence of enhanced connections, sending information back and forth between areas of the brain that they did not observe in the normally sighted group. These connections that appear to be unique in those with profound blindness suggest that the brain "rewires" itself in the absence of visual information to boost other senses. This is possible through the process of neuroplasticity, or the ability of our brains to adapt to our experiences naturally."[24]

Perception affects how we see ourselves and the world. Those who identify as more separate from their external reality tend to cling to their ego-self or Maya (illusion of self). Naturally, such a person puts their needs and desires higher than those of others. This creates a certain type of reality for a person with more self-directed characteristics. When our childhood needs are unmet, we become more self-involved as adults. When this becomes clear, we are empowered to trace selfish behaviors back to the root cause of neglect. This revelation acts as a catalyst in restoring the personal perception of health, assisting in a clearer view of reality.

ENERGY

The awareness of the universal life force energy seems to play a significant role in one's ability to understand the world around them. People who acknowledge the existence of an energy that connects all matter seem to connect with their environment and community more easily. However, those who do not perceive this energy live with a more pronounced sense of separation. One thing is clear: regardless of a person's take on this energy, our physical reality is made up of matter that's all around us.

SOCIETAL CONDITIONING

Our unconscious mental processes influence how we interpret information based on what we believe. This means the culmination of our lived experiences, cultural environment, and educational background act as filters that process what is happening now. These nuanced differences between our perceptions cause us to disregard ideas that don't align with our subconscious beliefs. If we believe our survival depends on being accepted in our immediate community, it is much more difficult to create tension by acting from beliefs that are not socially acceptable. Therefore, adopting the beliefs of the collective culture is the path of least resistance. What happens if we start to believe the collective culture is operating from a lower state of consciousness than is possible?

The irony isn't lost on me that I had an easier time "fitting in" to society when my life was a series of nuclear explosions and I presented myself as a dressed-up garbage can. All I had to do was put my mask on. When I decided to pursue wellness with the help of plant medicine, I became an outcast in my authenticity. Of course, I had a choice. The alternative was to descend into a socially acceptable state of consciousness and live a life of mediocrity. That particular choice didn't sit well with me. The fear of controversy often acts as a barrier to truth.

SPACE AND TIME

The way space and time interact with our senses and cognitive processes significantly impact our view of the physical world. Depending on our distance from an object, its size and shape may appear distorted. This is because of how light travels through space and how our eyesight interprets this information. Space influences our perception of depth. Objects further away appear smaller, and our brains use this information to calculate the relative distance between objects. Time impacts our view of reality as well. Time is a subjective perception that elements such as age, concentration, and emotional condition can impact. The passage of time might influence how we see events. Depending on our level of engagement with an event, its duration may appear shorter or longer.

Space and time are linked and can impact one another. In physics, we know this as the idea of spacetime, and the curvature of spacetime can alter the motion of objects and the rate of time dilation. In 2022, Frontiers in Psychology published an article by Birgitta Dresp-Langley. She posits:

"...consider consciousness as a form of creative energy beyond space and time, where specific cognitive abilities such as perception, memory or projective thinking and reasoning, although they may exploit conscious energy, need to be placed at a separate ontological level. An optimally expanded level of consciousness (by deep meditation or other mindfulness practice) would be equivalent to an expanded Self in a state of a deep sense of present, past, and future at one and the same moment in time".[25]

It has been my experience that pursuing mind, body, and spirit wellness has allowed for an expanded view of reality. In cultivating discernment, I question the societal norms I previously conformed to. I no longer seek advice outside of my inner guidance system. When I have a choice to make, I seek my own council first. In this way, I can avoid the trap of inviting other people's expectations into my decision-making process.

An example of this that recurs more frequently in my life is regarding health treatment options. I almost always do not take antibiotics prescribed by a doctor. There have been times when others strongly encouraged me to take antibiotics, but I resolutely declined. I've been able to heal myself of bronchitis and staph infections without the use of antibiotics. The ability to heal myself with natural products is empowering. Anyone can start hacking the reality matrix by using an expanded perspective of consciousness, energy, information, societal conditioning, and spacetime.

~ 9 ~

THE ISSUE OF EXPLOITATION
TODAY

American culture has many layers. Education, religion, online platforms, the entertainment industry, immigration, politics, and the criminal justice system are just some examples of areas within our society where sexual exploitation and crimes occur. Some areas of American society like to believe that sex trafficking only happens in foreign countries, but that simply isn't true. Sexual exploitation is a cancer affecting every layer of American culture. Underground sex involving exploitation is currently a $32 billion industry[26]. Is it possible our collective society is turning down the volume on this travesty? Are we allowing stories about the horrors that exist in the darkest parts of society to be silenced? The Roman Empire adopted a callousness towards all forms of sexual abuse before its demise.

Tim Ballard is one of the heroes of our time who has been fighting to save children sold into underground sex trafficking operations with his organization Operation Underground Railroad. Ballard is an anti-human trafficking activist and founder of one of the largest nonprofits fighting child sex trafficking in the world today. His mission was inspired by his former career as a special agent for the Department of Homeland Security as part of the Internet Crimes Against Children task force. Operation Underground Railroad draws inspiration from the history of the 19th-century underground railroad and the abolitionists who stood up to the injustice of slavery in the United States. Their fight is to end modern-day slavery, especially as it relates to child sex trafficking. They reach many layers of society that harbor traffickers.

One of his missions, "The Hidden War," tells the story of the organization's work in Ukraine to rescue orphans. Traffickers descended on the country in peril in what they were calling "Harvest Time." OUR and other organizations unearthed a pedophile network looking to traffic Ukrainian orphans to Mexico and around the world.

EDUCATION

Accusers in Redlands, California, charged 25 teachers with sexually abusing students in 1999. 24 years later, the story is coming to light as adult survivors come forward. In a recent CBS news interview, a former student described her experience with a well-liked and charismatic teacher. During a private examination, a 14-year-old high school girl's teacher raped her on two separate occasions. He threatened to kill her and her family if she ever told anyone. The former student stated at the end of the interview that "the wounds heal by taking action." Passivity is an action that our society cannot afford if we want to heal. Of the 25 teachers accused at the high school in Redlands, two were prosecuted. Laura Whitehurst pled no contest to six felony counts. She served six months of her one-year prison sentence. She is not a registered sex offender. Joel Koonce pled no contest to 16 felony counts. He is in prison and became eligible for parole in May 2023. No one at the Redlands Unified School District administration has faced any charges or lost their credentials or their jobs. With no admission of guilt, the Redlands Unified School District has paid out more than $41 million in settlements to students and their families for allegations of teacher sexual abuse in 23 cases. Nine more lawsuits are ongoing.

The Department of Education reports over 5.7 million children are victims of sexual abuse by their teachers in the United States alone. Here's the disturbing reality:

"The most comprehensive report about sexual abuse in public schools, published by the Department of Education in 2004, estimates—based on a 2000 survey, conducted by the American Association of University Women, of 2,065 students in grades 8 through 11—that nearly 10 percent of K-12 students have been victims of sexual misconduct by a public-school employee. Assuming that figure is accurate, this would translate into approximately 4.5 million children nationwide suffering sexual misconduct by public school employees, with about 3 million suffering physical sexual abuse—a number, according to the author of the study, Hofstra University professor Charol Shakeshaft, over 100 times greater than the physical abuse committed by Catholic priests, who, at the time the report was published, was undergoing a reckoning for the crimes within their ranks."[27]

This is only what is reported. The actual number of children abused in American schools is likely much higher. Places that are supposed to be safe, like schools, churches, and recovery homes, seem to have more elements of corruption. Small towns with houses set up to be safe havens for women recovering from alcoholism and addiction are being used as fronts for prostitution. One such case was reported in the Palm Beach Post in 2015. Lawrence Mower reported, "Kenny Chatman, with just one drug treatment facility, called Reflections Treatment Center, and several sober homes, is a bit of a player in the billion-dollar (sober living) industry. But may have taken it in a different direction: human trafficking, according to police reports." The very people running these homes and marketing themselves as saviors are trafficking a vulnerable population of human beings. It's modern-day slavery.

RELIGION

Religion is another area rampant with abuse. In 2018, the Maryland Office of the Attorney General investigated the Archdiocese of Baltimore and published a report of their findings in 2023.[28] Catholicism isn't the only religion with abuse. Religions throughout the world are harvesting the organs of babies and children to be used in rituals.

THE INTERNET

It's important to understand how the internet has made it easy for traffickers to access children all over the world and in ways that most people still don't fully grasp. From apps to social media to forums, our technologically advanced society has made room for every kind of sexual exploitation you can imagine. OnlyFans is a great example of a platform that exploits women who get paid less and less to do more and more. It also acts as a pyramid, wherein OnlyFans models can recruit other girls and make money from their earnings. This is how we've managed to normalize exploiting others.

In July 2016, in Maricopa, Arizona, 16-year-old Kat ran away from home after arguing with her parents. She had connected with a man named Rafael on her phone using Snapchat and an app called "MeetMe." He started grooming her by playing on her vulnerabilities. After introducing her to his friend Jesse Cisneros, he offered to give her a ride to Phoenix to get away from her parents. She climbed out of her bedroom window and got into his car. He covered her eyes; she was being trafficked and had no idea. Her parents filed a missing person's report. Meanwhile, Kat was taken to a hotel and forced to have sex with a stranger. This went on for a week before the police were called and rescued her. Many children are not so lucky.

Another daunting tactic used by traffickers is using video games to interact with children. ROBLOX is one of the most popular children's games in the world. It's an app that combines social commerce, social media, and gaming. ROBLOX allows users to play a wide variety of games, create games, and chat with others online. Two out of three children in the United States between the ages of 9 and 12 have played on this app. People Make Games, which is a British investigative YouTube channel that focuses on video game journalism, has criticized ROBLOX for missing moderation measures that should be in place to keep the players (children) safe.

ROBLOX has both open chat features and an internal "black market" for selling games, which leads to harmful or exploitative behavior without administrator oversight. Bad actors are using the content of the game to groom these young children—practices in the game act as a gateway to normalize explicit behavior. The characters often find themselves in areas of the game that feature underground dungeons. Players can enact scenes of rape. In May 2019, BBC News reported a story of a mother's preteen son being groomed by individuals in chat to send sexually explicit images of himself. In 2022, Court TV reported a story in which a 33-year-old Howard Graham convinced a 13-year-old girl in Topeka, Kansas, to run away from home in the ROBLOX chat. He picked her up and took her to Georgia. He's now facing rape and kidnapping charges.

HOLLYWOOD

The entertainment industry is also full of stories of exploitation. The #metoo movement helped to raise awareness around this issue. Some notable stars have offered their stories of exploitation, including former Disney actress Bella Thorne. Bella has been very public with her stories of sexual abuse from ages 6 to 14. In her book and on her social media accounts, she talks about being sexually explicit in her content because of her early exposure to sex. I admire her ferocity as she fearlessly faces public backlash while sharing her story and current mentality regarding her abuse authentically. She is one of the many survivors who leans on the encouragement of Maya Angelou's writings and speeches on how she overcame childhood sexual abuse. Bella said she felt like she was a liar by not sharing her story because she couldn't show people her truth. I can absolutely relate to this feeling. It feels like 90% of the people who know me haven't seen me until now. Bella has seen firsthand the connection and beauty she experiences with other people who have shared their stories with her and allowed her to see their pain.

Actress Rose McGowen wrote her account of being raped by Harvey Weinstein at the age of 23 in her memoir, *Brave*, published in 2018. During an episode of his Brotherly Love Podcast in 2023, actor Matthew Lawrence shared his story of sexual harassment in Hollywood. His agency sent him to meet an Oscar-award-winning director in his hotel room. When he got there, he was asked by the director to take his clothes off and perform sexual acts. If he did, he was told, he'd be the next Marvel super-hero. Matthew declined, and his agency fired him.

IMMIGRATION

Immigration is another layer of culture that has harbored criminals who sexually abuse vulnerable populations. Through-out the immigration process, women and children especially are vulnerable to abuse by traffickers during and after their journey to the United States. Dolph Lundgren produced a movie called *Skin Trade,* based on a true story about a group of women traf-ficked from Mexico to the United States who died while being transported because of a lack of oxygen. The movie helped raise awareness about this issue to the general public. More and more organizations and influencers are speaking up to help end exploitation.

Walk Free is a nonprofit organization that strives to disrupt the social norms and discriminatory attitudes that contribute to modern-day slavery. Their *Global Estimates of Modern Slavery* report published in 2022 states,

"More than 12 million of all people in modern slavery are children, and women and girls account for over half of them (54%). Migrant workers were three times more likely to be in forced labour than non-migrant workers. Modern slavery occurs in every country, regardless of wealth. More than half (52%) of all forced labour and a quarter of all forced marriages can be found in upper-middle-income or high-income countries."[29]

Considering recent world events at the time of writing, we have seen this play out in places like Ukraine. In 2022, weeks after the Russian invasion, UNICEF reported two-thirds of Ukraine's 7.5 million children had been displaced. Human traffickers see the tragedy as an opportunity for profit. On the site, E-International Relations, reporter Sylvain Keller wrote on June 15th, 2023, [30]

'...in 2022, the Ukrainian authorities arrested a gang that trafficked women and forced them into prostitution by offering them jobs in Turkey. In Hungary, local media reported several cases of car drivers who were offering transport and accommodation to Ukrainian people in exchange for sexual services. Authorities also warned that, in Slovenia, individuals were offering private accommodation to women from Ukraine in exchange for sexual services and household chores.'

Playing on a vulnerable group of people who fear deportation more than exploitation is a common occurrence in the time we live in. Evil runs rampant, and there is a desensitization of these occurrences that needs to be rectified.

~ 10 ~

AFTER SURVIVAL

In 2013, the FBI interviewed me in my home about a man I had crossed paths with during the years I lived in addiction to alcohol, drugs, and sexual exploitation. I learned that at that time, he still wasn't detained, and I should be cautious should I take part in providing information for their investigation. He was a sex trafficker who used profits to fund acts of terrorism. I was the only woman they were able to find to interview who wasn't either in prison or dead. Unfortunately, it's been normal for a long time in the United States for women caught in the cycle of prostitution after being trafficked to be arrested and labeled a criminal rather than rescued and rehabilitated.

In 2019, the police department in Phoenix, Arizona, started taking a different approach. In a frontline PBS special, an officer described the sex workers she encountered: "They span all ethnicities, all socioeconomic backgrounds, and all ages. We don't really call them prostitutes anymore, you know, we call them victims, and then we call them survivors. And we try to empower them a little as they move through that culture".

According to a 2020 report published by childusa.org, fewer than 15% of child sexual abuse survivors disclose crimes committed against them to legal authorities. The actual number of occurrences is much higher. Many don't survive, and many step into a life of further sexual exploitation because of unresolved traumas. I've yet to find a report showing even an estimate of how many survivors of sexual exploitation come forward to share their stories. The organization RAINN has a list of 1,500 different survivor stories. This is an incredibly small percentage of all the victims there are in the country. Colorado State University has a collection of stories from sexual assault survivors. They state on their website,[31] "Many victims and survivors of sexual assault feel that sharing their story, or even just portions of their story, has empowered them and has been a key part of their healing and activism." Not only does storytelling contain opportunities for personal healing and growth, but each story also echoes throughout our culture, bringing light into the dark corners of our shared reality. This provides for the healing of our families, communities, and generations. Just like the human body, society is interconnected.

Crimes that are suppressed from the public deteriorate our culture like a disease. I think our passivity to the crimes of humanity found in sexual exploitation acts on our cultural body the same way repressed emotions do on the physical body. If we can open our hearts to the real problems being faced every day because of exploitation, we can take on the total healing of our society needed in this era.

There are so many angles to tackle to realize the changes needed. Normalizing criminal behavior at the level of legislation and in the media is dangerous. Staying informed about what is happening at all societal levels regarding exploitation is paramount. We can all do our part based on our unique talents and backgrounds.

My own healing journey was hard to immerse myself in fully. Not recognizing my value for over a decade, I made many poor choices along the way. At one point, I married a man who performed acts of sexual abuse on me that were more violent than anything I remember experiencing working in the adult entertainment industry. Adjusting to life after trafficking is an ongoing process for everyone who experiences it. 16-year-old Kat received rehabilitation treatment from Phoenix's Dream Center, where she met other girls living at the Center who'd been trafficked for years. Each girl recalled being promised a world of material advantages like travel, safety, and nice clothes. The entrapment they all experienced was largely mental and emotional. Traffickers play on their victim's insecurities to get them in and keep them where they are. The experience of "coming to" years later and not even knowing who you are is a theme I resonated with as well. It took three years for Kat's traffickers to receive a sentence in a court of law. The three of them received prison sentences between 10 and 24 years and lifetime sex offender probation. Kat, meanwhile, has a lifetime of trauma to heal.

I've given you a lot of information, a lot of which is probably very hard to hear. What do we do once we have all this information about exploitation today? Where do we go? When we turn to each other to actively create a healthier environment to live in, we have a ripple effect that makes the world a safer place for everyone. As survivors share their stories, we can authentically meet them where they are and assist in the healing process with acknowledgment. Aftercare is the most important aspect of healing for survivors. It should comprise providing a safe environment to re-acclimate to life, focused education, therapy, and opportunity. Reintegration and healing are totally achievable, though unfortunately, this isn't the most common outcome at this point after someone goes through sexual exploitation.

DEVELOPING
SELF-COMPASSION

Forgiveness is one of the core aspects of recovery. Forgiving myself is simply illuminating the power each dark experience has given me to heal. Compassionately understanding my life choices, which led me down a destructive path, was the hardest part of my healing journey. I hated myself for years, but when I finally hit rock bottom, I started living in a way that allowed for increasing self-respect. Having adopted an attitude of radical responsibility, I believe in the power of choice.

On some level, I chose to experience everything I've gone through in this life. I still made the choice, even if it was subconsciously. It could be that some aspect of my being chose to engage in traumatic events to create a crucible of experiences that have allowed for extreme transformation. In a way, we all are responsible for transmuting our horrible experiences by healing past them, overcoming our obstacles, and growing into better versions of ourselves. This opportunity can be a gift. Collins Dictionary defines alchemy as "a power or process of changing one thing into another. Especially, a seemingly miraculous power or process of changing a thing into something better." Healing trauma by facing the darkest parts of my psyche is alchemy.

In Jon Hopkins' *A Gathering of the Tribe*, he states, "The fate of the world is in your hands. The key to this paradox lies within you in the feeling you carry that each of your actions, even your personal secret struggles, has cosmic significance. You will know then as you know now that everything you do matters."[32]

COMMITMENTS

One of the first steps I took towards developing trust within myself was to make small daily commitments and follow through with them. For instance, I would take my son on a mile-long walk every day at 4 p.m. The routine created a rhythm that felt safe. The healing process has allowed me to connect with others who have experienced similar pain. Learning to forgive myself is healing on a collective and personal level. Every time I choose to honor myself in ways I didn't during my years of enslavement to self, the healing I experience has a ripple effect. This is an opinion, but I've experienced it to be true. Seeing each of my actions as significant empowers me to make intentional choices that I can be proud of. This is how I cultivate self-appreciation. Each time I say no to spending time with someone I don't admire, I trust myself a little more and become stronger. My confidence increases when I refrain from participating in a group activity I don't see value in. The more that happens, the better equipped I am with the strength to help someone who reaches out for my help in their healing journey.

Overcoming my trust issues, especially with men, started with trusting myself. The micro commitments I could keep with myself, friends, and family eventually led to a high level of trust. I've explored the deepest parts of my mind and my higher self. Now, I recognize the divinity that exists beyond my physical makeup. The higher self knows, and the small self thinks. I learned how to access my higher self through my heart by exercising the power of my heart through meditation. I would visualize green light forming in my heart space, expanding, brightening, and protecting myself, my family, and my community. Now, when I listen to my heart, my questions disappear. I don't need to consult others for advice. I seek my own counsel first. True knowing is clear cognizance. When I align myself with this aspect of my being, I experience harmonic resonance.

I've had to build this foundation of trust within myself to embark on the next leg of the journey. That brings me to tell this story. I feel it is my duty to share the healing I've experienced with other survivors so they know they are not alone. There is a way out. Before sharing my story, the experience I had acted like an invisible sword that I knew deep down I wielded, but I could do nothing with. I can't fight exploitation from silence. I want to keep all these blessings. I do so by actively taking part in the conversation to end slavery, scary as it is. Silence was my way of participating in the game by giving permission to the passivity of our culture.

COMMUNITY

Coming together in a loving community is an invaluable resource. As I continue to transform and learn, I reach out to different groups that resonate with the new ideas I am exploring. I appreciate the long-distance communication the Internet provides. In the last couple of years, I've connected with people all over the world with shared interests. I regularly meet with other entrepreneurs, writers, healers, subject experts, and spiritual influencers. I was able to grow into this posture by first exploring the community at my local level. After engaging in local recovery programs, I eventually developed enough trust and confidence to branch out. I would encourage anyone struggling to find a supportive community to really pay attention to whom you admire and how they resonate with you. My body relaxes when I'm around the right people. This is what I look for when making new connections. The more of these connections I make, the more organic growth I experience.

~ 12 ~

INCORPORATING THE
SHADOWS

"Every man is two men; one is awake in the darkness, the other asleep in the light." ~Khalil Gibran

Darkness is the absence of light, what we don't know or see. Therefore, knowledge and truth allow for the transmutation of darkness into light. Truth conforms to reality. Knowledge stems from the Greek word *gnosis*, which means spiritual truth. In this way, knowledge, truth, and light interrelate. I uncover my light by carving away trauma and the associated negative behavior patterns. During my darkest days, I was never alone. I was never unsupported. The light inside me was always there. All I had to do was remember who I am. Romans 8:38 in King James' bible states, "For I am convinced that neither death nor life, nor angels, nor demons, neither the present, nor the future, nor any powers, neither height nor depth nor anything else in all creation, will separate us from the love of God." I find comfort in pieces of *gnosis* found in ancient texts like that. Love created me, and love got me out of that dark place. I can embody that love as I share my story.

Incorporating my personality's shadowy aspects involves transmuting negative emotions into productive thought patterns. I can start to put myself back together on the level of thought. I am becoming whole again, better than I was before breaking. The inner work reminds me of the Japanese method of repairing pottery called *kintsugi*. Broken pieces are glued back together using gold or silver powder. The result is an exquisitely unique design.

In early childhood, I believed I was unimportant. When blinded by this idea, it was a controlling factor that steered my ship into dangerous territory. Now that I know, I have the power to choose to redirect my thoughts. Everything in this life is a choice. Each choice either brings me closer to wholeness or further into separation. Each time an unhealthy thought arises, I can choose to let it go and replace it with something more productive. Old patterns continue to arise as I develop new beliefs; I still get tempted to run in the opposite direction of what my heart desires. It feels like a magnetic pull. This stems from that early cultivation of the belief that I don't deserve good things in my life because I lack value. Each time I react negatively to a promising situation, I recognize the old emotional responses and sit with myself. It takes a conscious effort to shut off the auto-pilot mode and remember who I am. The effect of the neglect was forgetting. When I pause in the middle of a triggering event, I can now parent my inner child with self-love. This starts with listening to why I am reacting negatively. Then, I can choose to accept and understand that dark aspect of my personality. I remind myself that I am worthy of blessings. Having embraced a mindset of gratitude, I'm able to continue to move towards the good things blossoming into my reality.

Opportunities to shed another layer of fear continue to arise, even now. The belief that I am unimportant separates me from love. Life has a way of triggering my insecurities when I least expect it. This is especially true if I dare attempt to have an intimate relationship with someone. I loved a man I had no reason to mistrust for years, yet it was more natural to assume I was not enough for him than to accept our connection. Jealousy and low self-esteem continue to plague me. Considering the level of betrayal I've experienced, it isn't surprising. However, I continue to hope and pray for the ability to be in a healthy, loving relationship one day as I work through feelings of hurt, rejection, jealousy, and disappointment.

Instead of acting on triggers, I try to sit with myself to acknowledge the inner child that is responding to hurt. I recall the emotional memory of expecting to be loved and supported by my biological parents. By ignoring this deep sense of betrayal, I would perpetuate the attraction to situations that cause these repressed emotions to take over. For example, since meeting my biological father, I've formed infatuations with a couple of men that reminded me of him. They were older, emotionally unavailable, and mostly hung out with me because they were physically attracted to me. When I recognized the pattern, I traced it back to the feeling of disappointment, shame, and heartbreak I had after meeting my father and realizing he wanted to sleep with me. That trauma was so strongly ingrained in my subconscious mind I was perpetually recreating it in my daily life. What I really wanted was unconditional love. I had to identify the root cause to heal this area of my life. From there, I could feel the pain to heal it and let it go. I was able to do this without the help of a psilocybin therapy session. Having learned how to deal with trauma in that setting, I instinctively know how to heal myself as layers rise to the surface.

Cultivating trust for myself and others is an ongoing process. Thankfully, now I can sit in meditation with my inner child and acknowledge her feelings. I tell her how loved and important she is and remind her where she is from—a place radiating with love.

If I do give into feelings of jealousy, rage, and judgment, the result is counterproductive feelings of shame. Shame creates a bubble that blocks access to the depths of a person's psyche. Anna Lembke states, "The pro-social shame cycle goes like this: Overconsumption leads to shame, which demands radical honesty and leads not to shunning, as with destructive shame, but to acceptance and empathy, coupled with a set of required actions to make amends. Increased belonging and decreased consumption results".[33] Closing the gap of separation by revealing the truth about my human nature is how I mend relationships with myself and others. I could wallow in self-pity when hurt or disappointed, but I understand how dangerous that is. The victim mentality is dishonest.

One of the more challenging experiences I've had to explore to escape my victim mentality was in my marriage. During the time I met my former husband and married him, I had zero impulse control and did not trust myself at all. His controlling nature was blatantly obvious, even to someone drinking a liter of vodka a day like I was. While he presented many red flags, on some level in my being, I knew his nature presented less of a threat than my volatility. I wanted to regroup far away from society. Some cabin in the middle of nowhere. That's exactly what

I got. That's why when I recall the marriage, I understand we were what each other needed at that point. I needed the space to recreate. He was my crucible. Taking radical responsibility for my thoughts, feelings, and actions allows me to reclaim my confidence and trust in my ability to make aligned choices.

Going forward, I look forward to the uncomfortable moments that trigger negative emotions to bubble up. I hope the deepest, darkest parts of my psyche feel comfortable enough to come out and play. As they do, I plan to continue to alchemize them. It's a lifelong process.

~ 13 ~

GRATITUDE AND REFLECTION

"Shunned for millennia across cultures as reprobate, parasites, pariah, and purveyors of moral turpitude, people with addiction have evolved a wisdom perfectly suited to the age we live in now."
~Anna Lembke

Over the years, a handful of people felt compelled to publicly humiliate me upon discovering aspects of my past in the adult entertainment industry. Those are the people I am most grateful for. Without their influence, I may not have been able to find my voice. Shame and fear overwhelmed me when I was exposed during those times. Coworkers, friends, and people in my community literally saw me naked. That's a nightmare most people only dream about, and I lived it. How beautiful that I don't have to be afraid of being exposed anymore; the worst has already happened!

Romans Chapter 8, verse 28 reads, "And we know all things work together for good to those who love God, to those who are the called according to His purpose." I fully believe this is true.

The power of gratitude keeps me centered. Appreciating everything I have, especially during life's biggest challenges, allows for a quickening of abundance. I am especially grateful for my two beautiful children. They are strong, healthy, and passionate. Their love and adoration of me are like nothing else. Many people in this world would give everything they have for that kind of love. They truly are my treasures, and every night, I thank them for letting me be their mother.

Owning my story is hard because the truth shatters illusions I've built throughout the years. When you own your story, you own your power. Each of us has an entire lifetime of experiences to weave into powerful stories of hope and redemption. We can all use our stories to impact people throughout the world. When we own our power in this way, connection replaces self-destruction. That connection creates love. The more love created in this world, the more healing happens. It's a ripple effect. I allowed myself to be broken so that I could heal and, by my healing, inspire hope and wonderment within those around me. Speaking my truth is how I cultivate the love that rescued me.

For all the words I've put down, I realize the nature of words masks reality. They have a blurring effect. Being and experiencing are closer to reality than doing and describing. Living in the moment is magical. Still, the act of storytelling is a necessary building block to creating the level of existence I know is possible.

This is truly an exciting point in time. As I find my voice and develop my message, the synchronicities that some call magic unfold at an accelerated pace. From far corners of the world, I reconnect with people who are awakening to who they are and the significance of the moment in time we inhabit.

When I look at devastating periods of my life, I see them as catalysts for miraculous growth and transformation in ways I could not have envisioned. Breaking down fear barriers is always productive. Everything I want is on the other side of fear.

A poem called *Footprints*, written by Margaret Powers, has always resonated with me from the time I was very young.

Footprints in the Sand

One night I dreamed a dream.
As I was walking along the beach with my Lord.
Across the dark sky flashed scenes from my life.
For each scene, I noticed two sets of footprints in the sand,
One belonging to me and one to my Lord.

After the last scene of my life flashed before me,
I looked back at the footprints in the sand.
I noticed that at many times along the path of my life,
especially at the very lowest and saddest times,
there was only one set of footprints.

This really troubled me, so I asked the Lord about it.
"Lord, you said once I decided to follow you,
You'd walk with me all the way.
But I noticed that during the saddest and most troublesome times
of my life,
there was only one set of footprints.

I don't understand why you would leave me when I needed You the most."

He whispered, "My precious child, I love you and will never leave you.
Never, ever, during your trials and testing.
When you saw only one set of footprints,
It was then that I carried you."[34]

There are so many people I want to thank for helping me on my journey. My brother has been solving the problems of the universe with me since the day I was born. Walking in their sovereignty, my sisters have always been a living example of what is possible. The dedication of my parents to show me the steadfast nature of unconditional love through their actions over a lifetime. The friends who have come alongside me stand shoulder to shoulder to witness the journey and take part in the change unfolding.

Many of the people I'm grateful for don't know me. I've been observing them from afar. Their truth sparked inspiration in me that dispelled my fear and helped me build the confidence needed to enter the conversation. I can only imagine the personal struggles they've endured to become their highest selves. All the bright lights in this world. How quickly our world is brightening! Each person's healing experience acts as a lens. If enough people share their perspectives on virtually any subject and their discoveries around it out of love, we develop a much larger lens through which to view our collective reality. The resulting *gnosis* gained sheds light on the world.

Exploitation, trauma, and addiction are the building materials I've gathered in this life. At first, I used them to build walls.

When I was tired of my confinement, I built a door. When I opened the door, I discovered wisdom and bliss. In blissful balance, I found Eden. In the now, which is eternity. I am grateful for that door because I'd still be lost without it. The best part of this story is it's only the beginning. My hope is that these words help other survivors remember that beautiful innocence of childlike wonder at the magic that still exists in this world.

Thank you for reading. I wish you well on your journey to reclaiming your highest, sovereign self, no matter what you've experienced in this lifetime.

REFERENCES

1. National Slavery and Human Trafficking Prevention Month. (n.d.). U.S. Department of Defense. https://dod.defense.gov/News/Special-Reports/0118_National-Slavery-Human-Trafficking-Prevention-Month/

2. Dr. Gabor Maté on How to Process Anger and Rage | The Tim Ferriss Show https://youtu.be/Yh1-y3TzSO4.

3. *Grooming.* (n.d.). Oxford Reference. https://doi.org/10.1093/acref/9780191834837.013.0179

4. *The Fantastic Fungi Film by Louie Schwartzberg.* (n.d.). Fantastic Fungi. https://fantasticfungi.com/film/

5. Labs, Sapien. "Neuronal Avalanches: What Are They and What Do They Mean? - Sapien Labs: Neuroscience: Human Brain Diversity Project." Sapien Labs | Neuroscience | Human Brain Diversity Project, August 29, 2022. https://sapienlabs.org/lab-talk/neuronal-avalanches-what-are-they-and-what-do-they-mean/

6. The Science of Brainwaves - the Language of the Brain | NeuroHealth Associates. (2019, December 2). Retrieved from https://nhahealth.com/brainwaves-the-language/

7. *What is Cymatics? Science of Visible Sound Explained.* (n.d.). Journey of Curiosity. https://journeyofcuriosity.net/pages/what-is-cymatics-how-to-explained#:~:text=Cymatics%20is%20the%20study%20of,of%20visible%20sound%20and%20vibration

8. MSE_Snippet.mp4. (2023, January 20). Roland Meinl Musikinstrumente GmbH & Co. KG. https://meinlsonicenergy.com/en/topics/flower-of-life

9. Kuriakose, & Soreng. (n.d.). THE GARDEN OF EDEN: CREATION AND CONSCIOUSNESS. *IJARIIE*, 7.

10. Eldridge, S. (2022, November 10). *Tree of Life | Meaning, Symbol, Biology, Name, & Movie.* Encyclopedia Britannica. https://www.britannica.com/topic/tree-of-life-religion

11. Maurer N, Nissel H, Egerbacher M, Gornik E, Schuller P, Traxler H. Anatomical Evidence of Acupuncture Meridians in the Human Extracellular Matrix: Results from a Macroscopic and Microscopic Interdisciplinary Multicentre Study on Human Corpses. Evid Based Complement Alternat Med. 2019 Mar 21;2019:6976892. doi: 10.1155/2019/6976892. PMID: 31015853; PMCID: PMC6448339

12. Anna Lembke, Dopamine Nation (USA: Dutton, 2021)

13. MacCallum, C. A., Lo, L. A., Pistawka, C. A., & Deol, J. K. (2022). Therapeutic use of psilocybin: Practical considerations for dosing and administration. *Frontiers in psychiatry*, *13*, 1040217. https://doi.org/10.3389/fpsyt.2022.1040217

14. Child Mind Institute. Reactive Attachment Disorder Basics (https://childmind.org/guide/reactive-attachment-disorder/). Accessed 2/21/2022

15. Grant, Joshua A. and Zeidan, Fadel. "Employing pain and mindfulness to understand consciousness: a symbiotic relationship." Current Opinion in Psychology, Volume 28 (2019): 192-197, sciencedirect.com

16. S Danho et al 2019 IOP Conf. Ser.: Mater. Sci. Eng. 564 012081

17. Joseph, Sonya. (2019). Sound Healing using Solfeggio Frequencies

18. Kučikienė D, Praninskienė R. Music's impact on the brain's bio-electrical oscillations. Acta Med Litu. 2018;25(2):101-106. doi: 10.6001/actamedica.v25i2.3763. PMID: 30210244; PMCID: PMC6130927

19. Jung J, Kim SK, Kim JY, Jeong MJ, Ryu CM. Beyond Chemical Triggers: Evidence for Sound-Evoked Physiological Reactions in Plants. Front Plant Sci. 2018 Jan 30;9:25. doi: 10.3389/fpls.2018.00025. PMID: 29441077; PMCID: PMC5797535

20. Jill Bolte Taylor, "Title of Ted Talk," filmed February 2008—my stroke of insight, 18:25, https://www.ted.com/talks/jill_bolte_taylor_my_stroke_of_insight?language=en.

21. Dass, R., & Das, R. (2011, November 8). *Be Love Now.* HarperOne.

22. *The wisdom of insecurity: a message for an age of anxiety.* (n.d.). Colorado Mountain College. https://cmc.marmot.org/Record/.b57954422

23. Stangor, C. and Walinga, J. (2014). Introduction to Psychology – 1st Canadian Edition. Victoria, B.C.: BCcampus.

24. *Brain "rewires" itself to enhance other senses in blind people.* (2017, March 17). ScienceDaily. https://www.sciencedaily.com/releases/2017/03/170322143236.htm

25. Dresp-Langley, B. (2022, January 10). *Consciousness Beyond Neural Fields: Expanding the Possibilities of What Has Not Yet Happened.* Frontiers in Psychology; Frontiers Media. https://doi.org/10.3389/fpsyg.2021.762349

26. Deshpande NA, Nour NM. Sex trafficking of women and girls. Rev Obstet Gynecol. 2013;6(1):e22-7. PMID: 23687554; PMCID: PMC3651545.

27. Errata Sheet, 2017–18 Civil Rights Data Collection Sexual Violence in K-12 Schools Issue Brief U.S. Department of Education Office for Civil Rights, December 2022, https://ocrdata.ed.gov/

28. Redacted Report on Child Sexual Abuse in the Archdiocese of Baltimore is Released by the Attorney General's Office. (2023, April 5). In *Maryland, the Attorney General (Press Release),* Maryland Attorney General. Retrieved November 2, 2023, from https://www.marylandattorneygeneral.gov/press/2023/040523.pdf

29. Global Estimates of Modern Slavery: Forced Labour and Forced Marriage International Labour Organization (ILO), Walk Free, and the International Organization for Migration (IOM), *Geneva,* 2022

30. Keller, S. (2023, June 15). *The Exploitation of Ukrainians: Additional Consequences of an Armed Conflict.* E-International Relations. https://www.e-ir.info/2023/06/15/the-exploitation-of-ukrainians-additional-consequences-of-an-armed-conflict/

31. *Sexual Assault Information | Safety | Colorado State University.* (n.d.). https://safety.colostate.edu/sexual-assault-information/

32. *A. M. (2021, December 8).* A Gathering of the Tribe | POWERFUL Short Film by Charles Eisenstein w/ Jon Hopkins & Aubrey Marcus. *YouTube. https://www.youtube.com/watch?v=XinVOpdcbVc*

33. Lembke, A (2021, August 24). *Dopamine Nation.* Penguin.

34. Zangare, B. (n.d.). *The Official Footprints In The Sand Page.* http://www.footprints-inthe-sand.com/index.php?page=Poem/Poem.php

About The Author

Sarah Lauren is an author and survivor who passionately pursues total wellness. Painfully shy and socially awkward, she prefers the quiet of country living while she recovers from these uncomfortable characteristics. Her debut, *Alchemizing Exploitation*, details her experiences with sexual exploitation and her journey of reclamation.

Sarah's mission is to empower survivors of exploitation to reclaim their personal sovereignty and remember who they are.

As a sex trafficking survivor herself, remembering who she is has changed her life forever. With radical responsibility, she understands that her purpose is to alchemize some of the worst experiences on Earth through storytelling. This has given her the ability to show others with similar backgrounds to do the same. Why? So, the millions of exploited worldwide can heal and embody the frequency of unconditional love.

4.5 million people worldwide are victims of forced sexual exploitation. 1 in 6 endangered runaways in the U.S. will likely become a sex trafficking victim. She is one of the fortunate survivors, but the real miracle was discovering a way to overcome the trauma.

It can happen to anyone, and Sarah is living proof of that. She also proves you can get out, create a better life, and help others do the same.

There is hope no matter what you've experienced in this lifetime.